DON'T BE FOOLED BY TIME MANAGEMENT MYTHS

TIME MYTH #1:

"I should get organized so I can get more done in less time."
No, getting organized will help you choose the most important tasks and get rid of, or let go of, the rest. The real benefit to getting organized is to have more free time.

TIME MYTH #2: "I can get it all done."

No one can get everything done. You can, however, by being organized, get most of it done and still have time left over for fun.

TIME MYTH #3: "I can remember everything."

If you free up your brain from the job of remembering, you can use it to be creative. The solution is to write things down in a pocket notebook.

PLAIN-SPEAKING, RIGHT ON THE MONEY, NO EMPTY PROMISES ...THAT'S LUCY HEDRICK AS SHE GETS YOU ORGANIZED BY USING THE REALLY SIMPLE FIVE-DAY, PROVEN SUCCESSFUL SYSTEM THAT CAN TRANSFORM YOUR HECTIC, OVERLOADED LIFE INTO ONE THAT IS TWICE AS PRODUCTIVE AND TEN TIMES MORE FUN.

FIVE DAYS
TO AN ORGANIZED LIFE

QUANTITY SALES

Most Dell books are available at special quantity discounts when purchased in bulk by corporations, organizations, and special-interest groups. Custom imprinting or excerpting can also be done to fit special needs. For details write: Dell Publishing, 666 Fifth Avenue, New York, NY 10103. Attn.: Special Sales Department.

INDIVIDUAL SALES

Are there any Dell books you want but cannot find in your local stores? If so, you can order them directly from us. You can get any Dell book in print. Simply include the book's title, author, and ISBN number if you have it, along with a check or money order (no cash can be accepted) for the full retail price plus $2.00 to cover shipping and handling. Mail to: Dell Readers Service, P.O. Box 5057, Des Plaines, IL 60017.

FIVE DAYS
TO AN
ORGANIZED
LIFE

LUCY H. HEDRICK

A DELL TRADE PAPERBACK

A DELL TRADE PAPERBACK

Published by
Dell Publishing
a division of
Bantam Doubleday Dell Publishing Group, Inc.
666 Fifth Avenue
New York, New York 10103

The case examples in this book are composites of some of the men and women who have taken my time management workshops. Any resemblance to a specific individual is purely coincidental.

We gratefully acknowledge permission to reprint:

Excerpt from Ellen Goodman, columnist, *The Boston Globe;* syndicated by the *Washington Post* Writers Group.

Excerpt from "The Importance of Play" by Eda LeShan. Copyright © 1981 by Eda LeShan. Originally appeared in *Woman's Day.*

How to Get Control of Your Time and Your Life by Alan Lakein. By permission of David McKay Co., division of Random House, Inc.

Excerpt from *Iacocca: An Autobiography* by Lee Iacocca and William Novak. Published by Bantam Books, a division of Bantam Doubleday Dell Publishing Group, Inc.

Excerpt from *Cheaper by the Dozen* by Frank B. Gilbreth, Jr., and Ernestine G. Carey. Published by Harper & Row Publishers, Inc.

The trademark Dell® is registered in the U.S. Patent and Trademark Office.

ISBN: 0-440-50215-2

Printed in the United States of America
Published simultaneously in Canada
February 1990

10 9 8 7 6 5 4 3 2 1

MVA

For Tom and Tod

Contents

Acknowledgments

I am indebted to many people for believing in me and this book. Thanks first and foremost to my husband, Tom, and my son, Tod, for their encouragement and support. I also thank Maury Hanson for giving me my first assignment on speculation for $50, and the Greenwich Writers' Group for suggesting I market my knowledge of organizing. Thank you, Jane Gubelin, for the joy of collaborating and for showing me how to enliven my prose, and Barbara Stretton and Judy Margolin for making me accountable for these chapters. Special thanks also to Pyke Johnson, who "doesn't read manuscripts," but who gives advice generously, often in the checkout lines of our grocery. I am further indebted to Judy Schedler for getting me started on my personal computer and to Bonnie Siverd for leading me to my outstanding agent and friend, Denise Marcil. Thank you, Jody Rein, my editor at Dell, for making my first book experience such a happy and positive one and Chris Benton for her substantive comments that made revising this book so invigorating. I thank my colleagues at the Greenwich YWCA for cheering me on every step of the way and John Tamerin for his friendship and strong beliefs in the principles contained herein. And finally, thanks to Jonathan Swift and all the Swifts and Hadsalls who came before, good writers all.

FIVE DAYS
TO AN
ORGANIZED
LIFE

Preface

My young son and I like to play a game of pretend. We imagine what it would be like to live in a world with unlimited time. It goes something like this:

"Once upon a time there was an imaginary world with unlimited time. In that world the sun is always up and there are no clocks. The people eat when they're hungry and sleep when they're tired. They play when they feel like it, and they work and learn when they want to."

Then my son chimes in: "The children don't have to be at school by a certain time. They don't even have to go to school at all." At this point I am quick to add, "When they get bored and want to go to school, they don't have to come home if they don't feel like it. The teachers assign homework, but the children have unlimited time to do it.

"In offices and manufacturing plants, men and women work on their projects when they want to, but nothing has to be completed by a certain time or date—there are no deadlines.

"In the households in this imaginary world, the homemakers shop when the cupboard is bare and do laundry when all the family's clothes are dirty. When a baby cries, a parent comforts it. When a teenage daughter needs to talk about her woes over her boyfriend, Mom and Dad can listen because whatever else they're doing can wait. There's always plenty of time."

My son and I always share a good laugh, but the fantasy starts to break down at about this point. With unlimited time, no one has to make any choices, so my son gets bored. If, however, I were playing this game with an adult, I might go on like this: "When a phone call comes in at the office, the person answering the call deals with the business of the call, large or small, from start to finish. It's never interrupting anything.

"When executives read the mail in their 'in' boxes, they attend to each piece, fully and completely, before moving on to the next. If they receive a 50-page report, they read it, from start to finish. If the next item they pick up is a letter that requires an answer, they write the reply then and there. If there's a bill to be paid, it's paid. And so on.

"If someone stops by the executive's office to ask a question, the visitor is dealt with right away. Or if she is interrupting the executive, she's told to wait until the executive has finished reading the 50-page report, hung up the phone, or answered the letter. After all, what's the rush?"

As the British economist Cyril Parkinson said, "Work expands to fill the time allotted to it." No problem. In our imaginary world there's never a shortage of time, and no one has to decide which activity is more important than any other. Alas, in the real world, everyone has 24 hours every day, everyone has deadlines, and many things happen simultaneously. We all have to make choices. And is that really so awful? One wonders if, in the world of unlimited time, teachers ever show up for school, students ever do their homework, the family cook ever gets dinner on the table, or the executive ever finalizes this year's budget—if anyone ever does *anything*.

Because you do have to do many things, you probably ask yourself questions like these every day: "What should I do first?" "What's most important here?" "What are my priorities?" It's the decision-making task, I feel, that makes us all yearn to get organized, to get on top of all the input into our lives. As individuals, even as children, we are bombarded with constant demands on our time. Spouses demand time, as do children, bosses, friends, communities, extended families, homes, pets, yards, cars, health, hobbies, and our spiritual selves. These demands rain down from all directions. The only way to make sense of the storm is to organize the demands.

Getting organized has become big business. More than 300 organizers, or personal planning aids, are currently on the market, and sales of organizers in 1989 are expected to exceed $200 million. Desk and office supplies manufacturers too are enjoying record sales, profiting from the sense of security we get from adhering to the old adage "a place for everything and everything in its place."

Time management seminars are prominent offerings on business training menus. Likewise, "get organized" articles appear in every consumer magazine with predictable regularity.

In spite of these aids, many of us are floundering. We complain that we have too much to do and not enough time. We purchase elaborate and expensive organizers, write in them diligently for several days, but soon abandon our good intentions for more pressing deadlines. Most of us—men and women, young and old—lead busy, active lives, but we're spinning our wheels: we're not moving forward, and we're not having much fun.

As a leader of seminars on time management and personal organization and a consultant to individuals, I have observed firsthand the personal logjams of hundreds of men and women. I've watched the same people learn and use my five-day system to take control of their lives and accomplish their goals. And most important, they're having lots of fun.

So, you want to get organized? *Five Days to an Organized Life* will help you do it. It works like this: Read one chapter a day, completing the exercises in each chapter before moving on to the next. You can choose to read the chapters over five consecutive days or opt for one day a week over five weeks to let each step become an integral part of your modus vivendi and to allow yourself time to collect tools and experiment with the process. At the end of five days, voilà! You'll be organized, *right here in this book*. More specifically, you'll know what you have to do and a logical order for doing it.

Five Days doesn't sail into psychological waters. It doesn't address your emotional blocks to doing what you say you want to do. It's not about the "inner game" of organization.

Instead, *Five Days* is a nuts-and-bolts—knit one, purl two—kind of book. I offer a system, a simple system, for reaching your goals. It works for any goal—personal, professional, social, even spiritual—and it's learned a little at a time over five days.

Before you start, understand that the five-day framework is simply a way to learn my organizing system. It's not meant to be a pattern you follow every five days in your life. Once you're organized, you'll spend less than 30 minutes a day staying that way—some days, less than five minutes. You'll spend the rest of the time doing what you want to do and having fun.

Why not begin today?

Introduction: What *Is* Organization?

☐ *Sam D. is a successful 36-year-old executive who would like to get married. All the women he meets through his job seem to be married or spoken for. He feels at a loss to spark up his social life, to enliven those lonely weekends and thus increase his chances of finding "Miss Right."*

☐ *Lorna R., at 47, is an empty-nester with three grown children finished with their education and on their own and a husband who is immersed in his own career. Time weighs heavy on her hands. She knows she wants to find something to do, either a job, volunteer work, or more education, but she doesn't know how to go about finding it.*

☐ *Helen and Dick M., empty-nesters as well as grandparents, want to move to smaller, more manageable quarters but are totally overwhelmed by the many decisions they face: Where should they move? What should they sell? What should they keep? And so on. While they stew in indecision, they become increasingly unable, physically and financially, to maintain their home.*

Each of these individuals is stuck. Though well educated and highly competent, they all feel overwhelmed by their problems and are unable to get out of first gear. They know what they want but not how to get it.

As a leader of time management workshops, as well as a consultant to individuals, business, and government, I have taught hundreds of persons, young and old, how to get "unstuck" without coming unglued—that is, how to get on with their lives and accomplish their goals, in an organized way, one step at a time. If you're stuck in a rut and dissatisfied with your life, then *Five Days to an Organized Life* will show you how to change it.

But first you have to understand what organization is—and what it isn't.

Stress has been the watchword of the 1980s, and business in stress management is booming. Solutions to excessive stress usually boil down to eating right, exercising, getting enough sleep, and *managing your time effectively.* Organization is time management, and time management is one part of stress management. As everyone knows, if you reduce stress, you will improve your health. So, in a very broad sense, organization is a way to a healthier, less stressful life.

Another word for getting organized is *planning.* Somehow planning has gotten a bad name—synonymous with *grind* or *drudgery.* The mere idea of planning usually makes the participants in my workshops grimace as if they're sucking on a wedge of lemon! My research tells me that those who recoil at the idea of planning have never learned the fun and creative way to plan. And of course, those who see planning as drudgery are complaining loudly, while those who find planning creative are too busy having fun. So you're left to form your opinions from planning's detractors. But stay tuned. *Five Days to an Organized Life* makes planning (or getting organized) fun.

Another way to look at planning is as *problem solving.* If you're stuck in a rut, you have a problem. The way you begin to solve the problem, in an organized way, is to make a plan for tackling it.

So, organization is time management, planning, and problem solving, to achieve your goals and lead a healthier, happy life. That's all well and good, but how do you go about getting, and staying, organized?

One of the first things you should do is to recognize what organization is *not.* Many of us find getting organized an impossible task because we're stymied by a raft of false premises about the process. We labor under certain widely promulgated delusions that foster in us unrealistic expectations and lead to self-defeat. I call these fallacies "organizational myths," those snippets of conventional wisdom (which could more aptly be called foolishness) that loom as stumbling blocks, set up insurmountable barriers, and cause us to engage in frustrating boondoggling. This book not only provides concrete steps to an organized, fulfilling life, but also debunks the myths that can only stand in your way.

ORGANIZATIONAL MYTH NO. 1: *"I can get it all done."*

This is the first, and perhaps the most important, myth. No one can get everything done. If reading this premise dashes your hopes for what you thought lay in store, by all means pass this book on to a friend with more realistic expectations.

You *can*, however, by being organized, get *most* of it done and still have time left over for fun. Which leads us to the second myth . . .

ORGANIZATIONAL MYTH NO. 2: *"I should get organized so I can get more done in less time."*

The real benefit of getting organized, and my personal philosophy, is to have more free time—time to do the things you've always dreamed of doing.

In our frenetic, fast-paced lives, we have 800 things to do. Someone who has the typical view of getting organized says, "I'm doing only 600 of these things. How do I get from 600 to 800, that is, get more done in less time?" (Seeking the answer to this question is one reason many people resort to buying those complex planners and organizers, as if cramming all 800 things into the pages of a planner will magically allow them to cram all 800 things into their lives.)

I feel that's not the right approach. You must choose the most important tasks and get rid of, or let go of, the rest. This gives you the free time to do what you enjoy.

ORGANIZATIONAL MYTH NO. 3: *"We are all born either organized or disorganized."*

People often point to me and say, "I bet you were born organized." That's nonsense. I had two organized parents and learned from their examples. More by osmosis, I would add, than by actual tutoring.

No one is born organized. People learn to be that way from their parents, teachers, peers, whomever. Likewise, anyone can learn not to be organized from these role models. However, if values like neatness, being on time, looking before you leap, and so on, were not part of your early learning, have no fear: you can learn to be more organized at any age, just as you can learn to operate a computer, to play an instrument, or to make a fluffy omelet.

Unfortunately, many people are often so busy that they dismiss the uneducated as "untrainable." Have you ever fired someone because he appeared disorganized? Have you ever taken the time to show him not only how to do the job but how to do it in an organized way? It is rare in an employment situation that a manager has the time to teach a subordinate how to get organized and therefore how to do the job more effectively. The manager has all she can do to fulfill her own responsibilities. The subordinate is left to sink or swim, and if he sinks, out he goes.

In any area of learning, inborn talent is a factor, and the same is true of organizing skills. I took piano lessons, and Van Cliburn took piano lessons, and I'm sure no one needs to be told who has more musical talent. People decide to become accountants because they are better in math than in English, and others choose the humanities because of their personal proclivities. Every field has experts as well as average players. Some people acquire organizing skills very easily; for others it's more difficult. But hundreds of men and women who have taken my workshops have demonstrated that anyone can learn to be more organized.

Using this book, you will learn how to get organized over five days, learning one step in the process each day. This framework embraces part of the book's philosophy—to break down large projects into manageable parts. So you can't cry the familiar excuse, "I'm so busy, I don't have time to get organized!" *Five Days* assumes you're already very busy and lets you learn just a little each day.

However, if you get harried, overloaded, or hopelessly lost—and everyone does now and then—you can return to the five-day framework, climb out of chaos, and get reorganized.

Be aware, however, that while this book will help you learn to get organized, it will not *make* you change your life. Being organized is nothing more than common sense in theory and reasonable self-discipline in practice. The difference between deciding to do something and doing it, that extra inch, is willpower. And willpower is not stimulated by a crack of the whip or a kick in the pants. Personal organization is learned and achieved more through the carrot than the whip, that is, by rewarding yourself for accomplishment. And that is precisely the subject of the next chapter, "Day One."

Now, before you read further, ask yourself a few questions: Why did you pick up this book? What's disorganized about your life? What are your time problems? What are your ruts? Be specific and write your answers below. When you get to the end of the book, you can look back and determine whether you have an organized, manageable strategy to solve your problems.

1. _____

_____

2. _____

_____

3. _____

_____

4. _____

_____

5. _____

_____

6. _____

_____

7. _____

_____

8. _____

_____

9. _____

_____

10. _____

_____

Rewards

□ *Peter R., in his twenties, is a foreman for a construction company. He makes a good salary but works a 60-hour week, sometimes more, driving to various job sites to check work progress, solve problems, or help in a crisis. He interviews and trains new workers, checks in regularly with the main office using the phone in his truck, and haggles with clients. Peter likes his work and has a bright future, but he complains he has too much to do, is exhausted, and drags himself through the end of every day. He falls into bed every night, often too tired to eat, only to start all over again the next day.*

□ *Sarah M. is a computer programmer for a utility company and single parent of two boys, aged three and five. Her day begins at 6:00 A.M.; she drops off the boys at day care at 7:30 and then commutes an hour by car to her job. Sarah usually eats lunch at her desk so she can complete her work and leave by 5:00. She collects her boys by 6:30; when they get home, she feeds them, bathes them, and reads to them. By then she feels totally drained, but she forces herself to sort through her mail and start a load of laundry before falling into bed.*

□ *Donald R., 52, is president of an international bank. He spends many days every month flying to domestic and overseas customers. He has a wife and three grown children he seldom sees. He sits on several community boards but attends fewer than one quarter of their meetings. At headquarters his days are an endless series of meetings, appointments, and phone calls. He often thinks of getting out of the rat race, but he never has time to give the idea more than a passing thought before his next appointment intervenes.*

The individuals in these examples are busy, productive, contributing members of society. They're not scatterbrained types who can't find their checkbook, who can't remember where they put the picnic cooler, or who lose the award they want to have framed. But they share one glaring characteristic: *they're not having any fun.*

What does having fun have to do with getting organized? A great deal. Day One of my five-day learning system is devoted to *rewards.* Those who thought getting organized would be nothing but drudgery can sit back, relax, and heave a sigh of relief: the first step to getting organized is to identify what you like to do for fun.

ORGANIZATIONAL MYTH No. 4: *"The satisfaction we receive from completing a job is the reward."*

When we complete a task, we usually feel a sense of accomplishment. However, if completing the task were reward enough, in and of itself, we would all do everything we set out to do. From designing a new model car to paying the bills, from defending a client in court to cleaning out the garage, from the stimulating to the routine, we would do all our work enthusiastically because the "high" resulting from the accomplishment would be too great to pass up.

But most of us are self-confessed procrastinators, either at certain times or when it comes to doing certain tasks. Peter R. puts off servicing his truck, even though it's vital to his work. In the back of his mind he's terrified the truck will break down on his busiest day, but since the nicks and knocks aren't too noticeable yet, he ignores the service schedule recommended by the manufacturer.

Sarah M.'s two sons need new winter clothes, but before she can think of shopping she must purge their closet and drawers and remove everything they've outgrown. Despite having free time on the weekends and a friendly neighbor offering to pitch in, Sarah procrastinates in favor of other urgencies.

Donald R. is no different. He wants to sell his vacation home in the Virgin Islands but continually puts off calling real estate brokers. There it sits, costing him maintenance charges and property taxes, which aren't nearly offset by occasional rental income.

The point is that there's fun work and not-so-fun work. For Peter, Sarah, Donald, and most of the rest of us, simply completing a job is not always enough. The solution? We must give ourselves a planned reward when we finish a job, particularly for more mundane tasks—

preparing our taxes, cleaning out the garage, returning phone calls, etc.

My research shows that many people don't reward themselves as a matter of routine. However, most of us are quite used to *giving* rewards to *others*. Think of training a pet, for example. When your dog sits up and lifts his paw to "shake," you reward him with a dog biscuit. Likewise, when he finds his bathroom in the yard rather than the house, you lavish him with praise and affectionate pats.

In parenting, too, we learn early on to reward our children's good behavior. When Sarah's boys behave well in the grocery store on Saturday morning, they are presented with a lollipop to enjoy on the ride home. For picking up their toys, putting their laundry in the hamper, hanging up their coats, and the like, they receive a small allowance once a week.

Giving rewards is no secret in business management, either. The managers and officers of Donald R.'s bank regularly receive year-end bonuses, as well as more personal gifts, to compliment their good work. Kenneth Blanchard and Spencer Johnson's *The One Minute Manager* advocates giving more frequent reinforcements, called "one minute praisings," to colleagues and subordinates to acknowledge work well done.

Why, when asked to "sit" and "shake," does you dog comply? Why do Sarah's sons hang up their jackets on the hooks near the back door? The reason was demonstrated by behavioral psychologist B. F. Skinner when he taught his laboratory rats to press a bar to get a pellet of food: an action that's followed by something pleasant tends to be repeated.

We must learn to give ourselves "pellets" for the same reason: so we will continue our good behavior, move ahead, and do what we want to do.

Give Yourself 15-Minute Rewards

In your daily life, what do you do when you stop working and take a break? How do you reward yourself when you finish a job? Take a minute to think of rewards you could give yourself in 15 minutes or less. Even though many of us can imagine finding time for a 15-minute break in an average day, I often encounter resistance to this exercise from the participants in my workshops. An elected town official complains, "My days are jam-packed. I'm always behind. I don't have enough time to do my job, let alone take breaks from it." Another resister, a woman bank officer, cries, "I don't have time to go to the bathroom!"

If you're having a similar reaction—if you never take a break, never give yourself a 15-minute reward—use your imagination. Pretend you live in a world with unlimited time and fantasize about nice things you would do for yourself.

When introduced to this exercise, many people encounter another stumbling block: What constitutes a reward? First and foremost, a reward must be just for you. It must relax you and divert you from your work, and it must be thoroughly pleasurable.

Second, a reward must not be simply another task masquerading as a reward. When beginning this exercise, one executive secretary exclaimed, "If I had 15 free minutes, I'd clean out the top drawer of my desk!" A task like this seemed like a reward to the secretary because she doesn't usually take time for it, but the truth is, of course, it's really work. To make that point, I asked, "How will you reward yourself after you've straightened the drawer?"

An author I know says that after a solid morning of working on her current book, she rewards herself by doing "diddly stuff," small, desk-clearing kinds of tasks that take up time but require less creative effort. She complains that she's having trouble getting down to the book. Like the executive secretary, the author is rewarding work with work. In talking about giving ourselves rewards for accomplishment, which also break our routine, I mean *fun* pastimes that are not part of your work. (For adults, play must *not* be work.)

In the space below, write down enjoyable things that you do, or would like to do, for yourself in 15 minutes or less.

15-Minute Rewards

1. _____

2. _____

3. _____

4. _____

5. _____

6. _____

7. _____

8. _____

9. _____

10. _____

11. _____

12. _____

13. _____

14. _____

15. _____

16. _____

17. _____

18. _____

19. _____

20. _____

Those who are used to rewarding themselves have no trouble completing this exercise, but if this is new behavior for you, take a look at the responses given by the people introduced at the beginning of the chapter.

Peter R. wrote the following:

1. Have a cup of coffee.
2. Skim through the sports section of the newspaper.
3. Walk around the block.

When he got a little more comfortable with the idea, Peter added:

4. Stop at the park and lie under a tree.
5. Skip stones on a pond.
6. Browse in the hardware store.

It's important to understand the difference between watching TV as a reward—that is, watching a chef concoct a recipe on a program you videotaped, tuning in a favorite weekly show, or relaxing in front of the news for 15 minutes—and passive TV watching, or plunking yourself in front of the TV and idly and restlessly flipping channels for 15 minutes. The former leaves you feeling refreshed and happy. The latter leaves you feeling ambivalent or dissatisfied.

Taking a nap is an activity that can be a reward for some but not for others. A 15-minute catnap leaves Donald R. feeling refreshed and reinvigorated. On the other hand, if you're someone who never gets enough sleep, to throw yourself on the couch in exhaustion for 15 minutes could make you feel worse.

Sarah M. knows the importance of looking at scenery other than her computer screen. She wrote:

1. Browse at the cosmetic counter of the drugstore across the street from my job.
2. Have a cup of tea away from my desk.
3. Call a friend to chat.

Donald R. confessed that he fantasized about these rewards:

1. Pick up the phone and call one of my children, just to chat.
2. Hold my calls and visitors, put up my feet, and close my eyes to meditate for 15 minutes.
3. Read a book, a spy thriller.

You're limited only by your imagination. Look at these excellent suggestions from a group of retired persons, which are also very appropriate for homemakers or anyone at home on weekends:

1. Watch TV or listen to the radio.
2. Put on a record and dance.
3. Play the piano and sing.
4. Pick flowers from the garden.
5. Look at nature through binoculars.

Taking Two or Three Hours for Yourself

I introduce workshop participants to 15-minute rewards first, partly due to my philosophy of starting out small and partly because, in reality, a couple of 15-minute breaks is a realistic expectation for busy people to carve out of their day.

However, you must find time for rewards of longer duration too. You might enjoy these rewards once a day or several times a week, during the day, evening, or on the weekends.

Two to three free hours may seem like a pipedream, but your imagination should have been stimulated by the first exercise; it will help you here, too. Below is a list of two- to three-hour rewards thought up by Peter, Sarah, and Donald.

1. Have lunch with a friend.

2. Exercise.

3. Go to a concert.

4. Take a walk, take my shoes off, and wade in a stream.

5. Ride a bicycle.

6. Go window-shopping.

7. Visit a museum.

8. Get a haircut, manicure, etc.

9. Have a massage.

10. Make love.

11. Do a crossword or jigsaw puzzle.

12. Write in a journal.

13. Invent a new recipe.

14. Read a book.

15. Sit in my backyard, doze, and contemplate the shapes formed by the clouds.

16. Go for a drive in a convertible with the top down.

17. Go to a spice or soap store and treat my nose to the variety of scents.

18. Sit on a park bench and watch the world go by. Sketch, if I'm in the mood. Have fun imagining a "secret past" about each passerby.

19. Go to a playground and swing on the swings. Try to remember what it felt like to be a child. Slide down the slide!

20. Go to one of those recording booths, the ones with the accompaniment for many songs, and sing my favorite rock and roll song.

Did you notice that the suggestions above became more and more playful? Play is necessary for good mental health, points out educator and family counselor Eda LeShan. Anyone who has ever observed children knows that you don't have to teach them how to play. It's inborn. (Actually, some child development experts have pointed out play *is* children's work—it's how they go about the business of learning.) But as we grow older, become educated, and take on more and more responsibility, do we lose our ability to play and have fun in favor of getting, earning, and achieving? Many of us do. "Although we need to work for physical survival," Ms. LeShan writes in *Woman's Day* magazine, "we need to play to make survival worthwhile."

It's important, however, not to get trapped in the semantics of rewards and fun. Many of us are lucky enough to enjoy the "fun" work that we do, at home or at the office, and that, of course, is "rewarding" in and of itself. Karen D., a high school guidance counselor, voices a common objection that I encounter: "I believe we should work not only for rewards, that the work we do should be satisfying, rewarding, and fun."

I agree, 100 percent, and I hope this book will show you how to achieve that end, in an organized way, one step at a time. Unfortunately, not all work is fun, and sometimes the only way to get through drudgery is to keep thinking of the reward that will follow. I don't know many individuals who actually enjoy paying bills, balancing the checkbook, shopping for groceries, cleaning the house, weeding out old files, and so on. For these tasks we need rewards.

But we also need rewards interspersed between tasks that *are* enjoyable. We need rewards because "all work and no play makes John a dull boy" or Jane a dull girl. As I said before, rewards increase productivity by boosting our morale and recharging our batteries. We feel refreshed and ready to tackle the next challenge. Rewards also provide us with a balanced life, a life that includes work *and* play.

In the space below, write down pleasant things that you do, or would like to do, for yourself in two to three hours.

Two- to Three-Hour Rewards

1. _____
2. _____
3. _____
4. _____
5. _____
6. _____
7. _____
8. _____
9. _____
10. _____
11. _____
12. _____
13. _____
14. _____
15. _____
16. _____
17. _____
18. _____
19. _____
20. _____

Exercise as a reward needs to be considered carefully. For some people it is work. They do it because they know it's good for them because it helps reduce stress, because in doing it they burn extra calories, and so on. For others, jogging, 90 minutes of brisk tennis, skiing, and the like are pure pleasure and escape from work. Only you know what you value as a reward. And the values you apply must be your values, not someone else's.

So, going shopping is a reward if you don't have a list of 10 items to buy. Reading a magazine is a reward if it is not a trade publication, even if you don't get around to your trade reading as much as you'd like to. And creating a recipe is a reward provided it's not done in haste for unexpected company.

Imagine a Whole Day Off!

Finally, in the space below, write down nice things that you do, or would like to do, for yourself in the better part of a day.

Day-Long Rewards

1. _____

2. _____

3. _____

4. _____

5. _____

6. _____

7. _____

8. _____

9. _____

10. _____

11. _____

12. _____

13. _____

14. _____

15. _____

16. _____

17. _____

18. _____

19. _____

20. _____

At first, giving yourself a reward that lasts for the better part of a day could seem like a formidable task for somone who's new at this. Becoming comfortable with rewarding yourself, in small chunks of time or large, is a matter of practice. A little later in this chapter, I'll show you how to get started in determining when to take reward breaks and for how long.

Again, to help you get started, look at the whole day rewards suggested by Peter, Sarah, and Donald.

1. Take a hike and a picnic.

2. Read a book at the beach.

3. Go out to lunch and a matinee.

4. Go out to dinner and a movie.

5. Spend the day at a spa.

6. Go antiquing.

7. Take a boat excursion.

8. Go fishing.

9. Spend a day browsing at a public library.

10. Play golf.

11. Paint a picture.

12. Visit my family.

13. Stay home, curl up in front of a fire, and look at art books.

14. Go to the zoo.

15. Take a ride in a hot air balloon.

16. Tour a winery and taste its wares.

17. Make a snow sculpture, go tobogganing, and warm up in a hot tub with a cup of hot cider.

Did reward number 13 in the preceding list appeal to you? If so, suggestion number 15 from the list of two- to three-hour rewards probably did too. I have a friend who works full-time, and though she is married, she calls herself a "Saturday widow." Her husband's work requires him to visit clients on Saturday.

"I love my Saturdays," she says. "I don't have to get dressed if I don't want to. I don't have to go out if I don't want to. I can stay home all day and unwind."

A minister I know talks about "Sabbath time," or quiet time when we let go, free ourselves from everyday demands, and just let ourselves be. "The pace of our lives is hectic and stressed," she says. "*Not* working on Sunday is no longer efficient. In today's society some *have* to work. Business seems to proceed as usual. The stores beckon us to their sales. Meetings have to take place on Sundays because there's no time to meet on weekdays. Even when one is free to engage in so-called recreation, one feels the *obligation* to play at something because it's a day off. One must accomplish, fill the time with activity. Just plain relaxing would be considered boring, wasting time.

"I recommend wasting time, gloriously, appreciatively, attentively," she continues. "I want to call a halt to all our frenzied, driven activities. I want to shower everyone with gentle time, quiet time . . . Sabbath time."

Lest your rewards become too active, too busy, and resemble too much the pressure-cooker style of your nine-to-five life, be sure that your reward lists contain a balance of truly quiet rewards.

This does not mean, of course, that all the best rewards are those enjoyed by yourself. When you have lunch with a friend, and it's not a "working lunch," hopefully that's a reward for both of you. If you like to visit the zoo, it's a reward if you go by yourself or take along one of your offspring. But it's *not* a reward if you take your three kids, plus three from the neighborhood, are fresh out of Band-Aids when two skin their knees, and don't get halfway around the park before every-one is tired, cranky, and prone to tantrums.

Your first efforts at rewarding yourself may involve some trial and error. The best-laid plans for rewards can go awry, and you might have to fight a tendency in yourself to mix business with pleasure. Rest assured that learning new behavior, such as rewarding yourself, takes time. The loudest complaint by the people who take my organizing workshops is that they're too busy to have any fun. But rewarding yourself *is* very easy to learn. After all, we're talking about putting some fun into your life!

Try this simple exercise to prove that to yourself. Fold your hands in your lap. Is your right thumb or your left thumb on top? Now fold your hands so that the other thumb is on top. How does it feel? A little awkward at first, but not too difficult. Learning to use rewards is no harder than this. The following examples should prove inspiring.

Peter R., the construction foreman, agrees to give rewarding himself a try. After visiting four construction sites, he drives to a park he passes daily in his travels. For just 10 minutes he sits on a bench and watches birds, squirrels, and the wind in the trees. A glance at his watch tells Peter it's time to check in with the main office on the radio in his truck and to visit the lumberyard.

Peter is surprised and then pleased to find his afternoon goes more smoothly. He processes orders for materials at the lumberyard quickly and efficiently and doesn't have trouble remaining focused on the task. As a reward for accomplishing two and a half hours of ordering with dispatch, he stops at a corner store for coffee and an apple (he has skipped lunch). Instead of trying to eat while driving his truck through traffic, which can be not only messy but dangerous, Peter returns to the same park for a few minutes to eat his snack.

He returns to the main office at 4:30 P.M. to face mounds of paperwork and many phone calls to return. But again, refreshed from his reward, from pausing after completing a job to do something pleasant for a few minutes, he plunges into the piles of phone messages and other paper.

Sarah M. feels her reward choices are more limited. She sits at a computer terminal along with almost 50 other programmers, separated by partitions but not walls and doors. She hears not only her own phone ring but everyone else's as well.

The office isn't near any parks; it stands in a concrete industrial park across a divided highway from a rather limited shopping center. Nevertheless, Sarah can think of some ways to escape from her computer.

Sarah can take a coffee break in the employee lounge, and she can eat lunch away from her desk in the company cafeteria. There are sidewalks in the industrial complex, and a leisurely stroll (notice I did not say "an aerobic walk") gives Sarah some fresh air and a chance to stretch her legs. In addition, there's a traffic light that allows pedestrian crossing to the shopping center across the highway.

At first Sarah is very anxious about using rewards. She's afraid that taking time out will simply make her workday longer. Firmly tied to her children's day-care schedule, she can't afford to be delayed in leaving work.

Sarah ventures at first to the employee lounge for just five minutes in mid-morning. Later the same afternoon, after finishing a large project, she visits the lounge again. Gradually she extends her breaks. By Friday Sarah realizes she will complete her week's work by lunchtime. She celebrates by getting her hair cut at the salon in the shopping center. Although she needs a haircut, she loves the feeling of being pampered and knows she deserves this reward for finishing her week's project a little early.

Donald R., with the privileges of rank, learns quickly to take a break within his own office suite. His administrative assistant can hold his telephone calls; he can close the door and/or the window blinds and read the sports page, listen to an audiotape, or take a nap. He is resistant, however, to rewarding himself by leaving his office. All lunches must be working lunches, and he would never think of using the employee fitness center the bank provides. Nevertheless, like Peter and Sarah, Donald discovers that after rewarding himself he's more alert. He used to fight heavy eyelids in late afternoon. Now, after a reward, he feels revived, his energy replenished.

Donald's experience comes as no surprise to those who have studied productivity in the workplace. Engineering psychologists have demonstrated again and again that the appropriate placement of rest periods increases work rates, reduces errors, reduces unofficial breaks, and leads to higher worker satisfaction. These conclusions are obvious to most of us, so much so that one could argue it's common sense. Even so, we often don't practice what we would gladly preach.

After Completing a Task, Enjoy a Reward

Even if you don't work on an assembly line or for an employer who mandates regular breaks in the workday, you can learn to identify logical times during the day to reward yourself. The trick is to take a break whenever you've finished a job or part of one. And don't delay. Rewards that are too far removed from the job that warranted them lose their impact. (I'm not advocating "instant gratification" as a way of life but as a way to accomplish what you want.)

For example, when a long meeting adjourns, you might take a walk around the block. When you finish the first draft of a five-year marketing plan, it's time to have lunch with a friend. And when you close the footlockers that will outfit your sons for summer camp, it's time to have a cup of coffee and read your current choice of fiction.

As it is said in criminology, and in parenting, the punishment should fit the crime. Likewise, the reward should fit the accomplishment.

Take a moment to complete the exercise below. Think about the work that you do every day and list some of the tasks in the column on the left. On the right, list a suitable reward. And don't confine yourself to 15-minute rewards.

Tasks with Rewards

Tasks	*Rewards*
1. _____	1. _____
2. _____	2. _____
3. _____	3. _____
4. _____	4. _____
5. _____	5. _____
6. _____	6. _____
7. _____	7. _____
8. _____	8. _____
9. _____	9. _____
10. _____	10. _____

Look at the imaginative rewards used by some creative people who've taken my workshop. (If you like any of their ideas, be sure to add them to your list.)

1. I finished researching, interviewing, and selecting a financial planner.
2. I finished planning a three-day sales conference.
3. I asked my boss for a raise.
4. I finished a difficult telephone call to a manufacturer, complaining about and demanding replacement for a defective product.
5. I finished writing a chapter of my novel.
6. I finished a pile of mending.
7. I finished my Christmas shopping.
8. I registered for an exercise class.
9. I made five appointments with prospective clients who need life insurance.
10. I signed a lease on a new apartment.

1. I had lunch with a friend.
2. I saw an art exhibit on my lunch hour.
3. I took a walk around the block.
4. I flipped through my favorite cookbook.
5. I went ice-skating.
6. I watched a TV talk show with a cup of tea.
7. I relaxed at home with a fire, the stereo, and a book.
8. I called a friend.
9. I bought myself a steak, a bottle of wine, and some fresh flowers.
10. I played golf.

Make Time for Fun on Weekends

We need to use rewards on weekends too. Many of my workshop participants complain that their weekends are as frenetic as their weekdays. Saturdays are devoted to endless errands and household chores, coupled with a whirlwind social life. I know a woman who takes personal days, so-called "mental health days," and spends them scurrying around like a madwoman who's determined to catch up on every chore she's ever put off. I'm sure I don't need to tell you that she returns to work more frazzled than when she left for her day off.

Still, people have difficulty rewarding themselves on weekends, especially single parents or two-career couples with children. They often feel that since they are away from their children so much during the week, taking time to reward themselves on the weekend would be tantamount to criminal negligence. Unfortunately, if you ask these parents how they feel after a weekend of total devotion to home and family, they say "burned out" and "dissatisfied."

Harry Corsover, Ph.D., a therapist specializing in stress management, sees many parents in his practice who feel that if they put themselves first, they're ignoring the needs of their family. He advocates what he calls "responsible selfishness."

"If we don't take care of ourselves—eat right, get enough sleep, exercise, *and* reward ourselves with enjoyable pastimes—how can we expect our children to learn this behavior?" Dr. Corsover asks. "When we deny ourselves interruptions from work and parenting, we're telling our kids that life as an adult is all work and Mom and Dad are all-sacrificing."

As one junior high school teacher said at a workshop, "Weekends are a lot like summer vacation for teachers. There's lots of work you have to do—around the house, for your family, or preparing for next fall—that you've put off until summer vacation and lots of fun pastimes you've waited all year to have time for." Weekends, and summer vacations for teachers, should have a balance of both.

Peter R., because his working hours during the week are so long, must often join his bosses to meet with new or prospective clients on Saturdays. Then he has a long list of what I call "life maintenance chores"—laundry, grocery shopping, bank deposits, new shoes to buy, haircut, etc.—to do. He also does a lot of passive TV watching out of sheer exhaustion. But once again, there's a glaring omission: rewards, or fun.

Peter remembers how rewarding himself during a workday increased not only his productivity but also his feelings of self-satisfaction, and he resolves to continue this practice on weekends. He takes a minute to identify when he will finish a task and the suitable rewards that will follow.

After two appointments with new clients at the proposed job sites, Peter stops at the park to eat his lunch. On an impulse he goes to a nearby pay phone and calls two friends to suggest spending the evening together. The first is busy, but the second buddy is free. They agree to meet later that evening for pizza.

Peter feels exhilarated because he's done something he's often only thought of doing: calling a buddy and spending an evening with him. It's something as simple as a phone call and yet so easily dismissed when Peter's so exhausted. Peter gives himself a reward for his initiative, a trip to the hardware store, just to check out what's new.

Peter breezes through the afternoon's errands and realizes another important aspect of a planned reward: anticipating that reward, that fun, that time off, gives us fuel to get our work done.

Sarah M. usually devotes her entire weekend to life maintenance chores and being with her kids. She looks forward to the end of the workweek and the end of thinking about computer programs, but by Sunday, after constant errands, housework, and kids, she's anxious for Monday morning to return. Understandably, Sarah is puzzled.

Once again, what's missing from Sarah's weekends is time for herself. At first she's convinced she must be with her children all weekend and that there aren't any opportunities to be away from them anyway. With some gentle prodding from other workshop participants, Sarah realizes there are loopholes in her logic. Instead of declining when the boys across the street invite her sons to play, she can accept, and Sarah gains a few hours of freedom for herself. She can hire baby-sitters. And she can take turns watching the children with other mothers.

Sarah identifies appropriate times to reward herself in between and at the end of chores she wants to accomplish on the weekend. Although she starts out small—relaxing with a fashion magazine and a soft drink, taking her sons to a diner for dinner instead of cooking in—she notices she feels less impatient and irritable.

Months later I ran into Sarah while shopping. She told me she and two friends now have Saturday night subscriptions to a local theater series. Sarah says it's her reward for coping as a single parent with a full-time job. Amen.

Donald R. often wastes half of Saturday returning from business travel. And even if he's home on Friday evening, he has one arm in his briefcase for a large part of the weekend. When there's no more bank work he can do, or when he's too exhausted, Don vegetates in front of the television, restlessly flipping channels with his remote control unit and drinking highballs he loses count of.

Remember the 15-minute rewards Don thought of? The other men and women in Don's workshop suggest, as a starting point, that he expand on those rewards and incorporate them into his weekend. Don agrees to reward himself by going to a bookstore and selecting a spy thriller and by taking his wife, son, and daughter-in-law out to dinner.

When Don is given permission to fantasize about rewards he'd like to have, it's as if a floodgate is opened. He decides to attend the U.S. Open Tennis Tournament instead of just watching it on TV, and he gets tickets for a ballet. He goes for his own enjoyment, not to entertain business clients.

His family can't resist teasing him about his new behavior, but one and all agree weekends are now more enjoyable. Slowly but surely Don is becoming less anxious and less inclined to fill his unstructured weekend time with bank work.

When Peter, Sarah and Donald gave themselves some rewards, that is, fun, they increased their productivity and thereby gave themselves time for more fun. From their desire to get organized, they took a "leap of faith"—they took the time for some rewards instead of thinking about all the reasons they didn't have the time.

Taking small breaks from her work increased Sarah's effectiveness and thus netted her time off at the end of the week. Peter experienced the same thing, which gave him the time and energy to go out with a friend for an evening. Donald, who thought he never had time off from bank work, went ahead and bought ballet tickets and found he certainly had time to go . . . the time he used to spend drinking highballs and watching TV.

Imagine your next weekend filled with a balance of the work you have to do and rewards you want to do. As you did on page 27, list some tasks you hope to accomplish in the coming weekend. Beside each one, list a suitable reward.

Weekend Tasks with Rewards

Tasks	*Rewards*
1. _____	1. _____
2. _____	2. _____
3. _____	3. _____
4. _____	4. _____
5. _____	5. _____
6. _____	6. _____
7. _____	7. _____
8. _____	8. _____
9. _____	9. _____
10. _____	10. _____

Congratulations. You've completed the first day toward getting yourself organized. We talked about rewards and playing and having fun, which is what you'll have time for when you get organized. But the way to get organized is to give yourself a little fun along the way. All that remains is to practice the first lesson: for reading this chapter and completing the exercises, give yourself a reward.

DAY 1

1. Start with 15-minute rewards.

   Productivity increases, allowing you to...

2. Take two- or three-hour rewards.

   Self-satisfaction leads to increased vitality, which allows you to entertain the possibility that you can...

3. Take a whole day off for yourself.

   Now you're beginning to see that time for fun *can* be there, so you can look at your typical day and...

4. Match tasks with appropriate rewards.

   If you can do it on weekdays, surely you can...

5. Take time for fun on weekends.

Give yourself a reward!

Bite-size
Brainstorming

□ *The Communications Department of a large consumer products company designs and produces brochures to explain the company's many community outreach programs—sponsoring a running marathon, a management intern program for students at the state university, and a scholarship program for black youths entering medicine-related fields. These brochures sit in cartons stuffed under tables in the department's offices. The managers never decided who was going to read these brochures or how the department would distribute them. Furthermore, upper management priorities changed. The company is now funding programs for the arts. The morale in the Communications Department is low.*

□ *A group of high school students from a church in a small town in the Midwest want to raise funds to go on a trip. They decide to hold a car wash one Saturday in the church parking lot. That morning half a dozen willing scrubbers show up with hoses, soap, buckets, and sponges, but find, much to their dismay, the water pressure from the outside church faucet is just a trickle. Only a few cars show up for the lengthy wash because the kids forgot to publicize their event. Needless to say, the church youths fell short of their expected profits and felt very discouraged.*

□ *A young bachelor physician, desiring some security for his condominium and companionship for himself, brings home a black Labrador retriever from the local animal shelter. The doctor invests in a full complement of doggie equipment, a visit to the vet, and the appropriate licenses, and he and his Lab have a great time getting acquainted over the first weekend. On Monday evening the doctor returns to his condo late at night after a long day's work to find that the Lab, out of frustration over his master's prolonged absence and a space too small in which to roam, has chewed the place to bits. The doctor returns the Lab to the shelter and begins the lengthy, and costly process of repairing his furnishings.*

What happened in each of the three examples above? In each case the group or individual plunged into a task *before* thinking about it. These people failed to brainstorm, to take a small amount of thinking time that would have saved a great amount of doing time—and money—in the long run. You can never plan for every contingency, but you can go a long way toward planning for most of them.

On Day One, you learned how to use rewards to increase your productivity and therefore save time. On Day Two you will learn to use one of the most important timesaving techniques at your disposal—brainstorming. The first and most important step in planning, brainstorming is the one most often skipped over. When you omit brainstorming and start a project, frequently you encounter stumbling blocks you didn't take time to anticipate, as our examples showed.

Brainstorming—which means, literally, to "storm the brain," to produce a flood of ideas—is the first step in problem solving. People in all areas of life use the brainstorming technique. Companies come up with ideas for new products and names for those products by brainstorming, schools generate new areas of curriculum, and concerned groups of citizens create solutions to community problems through the intuitive process of brainstorming. Most of us have participated in such a brainstorming session where a group sets out to solve a problem through the spontaneous contribution of ideas from all members. It's an effective technique and you as an individual can use it just as successfully.

Bite-size Brainstorming for a Committee of One

Why do *you* need to brainstorm? Because you have goals to achieve, tasks to complete and problems to solve, and they can all seem overwhelming.

When you brainstorm by yourself, you're looking for a spontaneous flow of ideas, but more specifically, you're looking for the smaller parts of the whole. That's why I call it "bite-size brainstorming." The object of brainstorming when you're trying to get organized is more than just free-associating—the purpose is to break down a goal into its smallest parts. Organizing consultants liken this strategy to eating an elephant—one bite at a time. The goal that seems unattainable when looked at as a whole (so much so that you're likely to abandon it altogether) becomes manageable when broken into its bite-size components.

In its simplest form, bite-size brainstorming means making a list. It also means breaking your goals into smaller, more manageable subsections that, one by one, can be accomplished. Not performing this first important step may be one of the reasons why you've failed to complete goals in the past.

The list you make may not be complete, but that doesn't matter. What matters is that you've started—and you're moving.

That's the trick: brainstorming each step of your elephant-size goal down into smaller and smaller substeps until you finally say, "That's it. I've got it. I can do that. I want to do that. I'm going to do that." If you haven't achieved those feelings, you haven't broken it down far enough. Go back and break it down some more.

My workshop participants often point out other situations they've encountered where breaking down something large into its smallest components is the prescribed strategy. A clinical psychologist told me of his work with phobics.

"When treating a patient with an irrational, excessive fear of spiders, for example, we start with the most minimal exposure," he explained. "We might show the patient a color photograph of a beautiful rose garden, which also includes a tiny spider."

A retired computer programmer offered another analogy. The earliest computers, developed in the late 1930s and 1940s, were based on a binary number system of 0 and 1. That meant that computers understood only on or off, white or black, yes or no; they were capable of looking at only two choices at a time, before presenting two others, based on the first choice. Each time the programmer chose "yes," he was presented with another yes or no choice. He had the same alternatives if he chose "no," ad infinitum in an endless expanding progression like this:

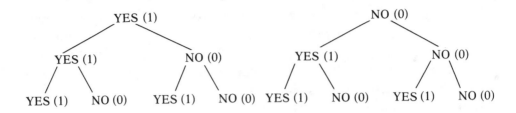

Computers made these decisions very fast, and indeed today there are operating systems, or shortcuts, that do it even faster. But whether or not you understand computers, the programmer was correct: his job was to eat elephants one bite, or decision, at a time.

ORGANIZATIONAL MYTH NO. 5: *You can't see the woods for the trees.*

Paradoxically, when you brainstorm to break up something large into smaller pieces, you really *are* looking at the big picture. Bite-size brainstorming as a step in the organizing process is often skipped because people haven't understood the importance of looking at the whole elephant. In their haste to get more and more accomplished, they plunged into a pile of tasks without having any idea how many parts there are between the elephant's tusks and its tail. The result? They never finish the elephant.

If you bite-size brainstorm first, you give yourself the opportunity to think of every possible contingency, every detail. This way you won't miss anything or forget something en route to getting it done, and you'll be better prepared for the unpredictable bites ahead. In other words, brainstorming saves time.

Before you begin to brainstorm as a committee of one, of course, you have to identify your goal (or elephant).

Start with a Goal

Select any goal, personal or professional, that you want to accomplish. Here are some examples of goals from my workshops:

1. Clean out the attic.

2. Take a trip to Europe.
3. Double profits in two years.
4. Change careers.
5. Get a dog.
6. Make a will.
7. Start a community task force.
8. Raise $10 million for capital improvements.
9. Buy a vacation home.
10. Find baby-sitters.
11. Apply to colleges.
12. Plan a family holiday.
13. Have a block party.
14. Improve my marriage.
15. Expand my business to a second location.
16. Get organized.

Anything you want, need, or have to do is a goal, and hopefully it truly is *your* goal and not someone else's goal for you.

If your boss says you must deliver the annual report by February 1, delivering that report is your goal, assuming you want to keep your job. If you want to buy a sports car, that is your goal. If your parents want you to go to college right after high school, but you want to work for a while and take some time to think about your career direction, going to college is not your goal right now. Instead, your goal is to resolve your conflict with your parents.

Some people complain they haven't any specific goals, that they don't know what they want to do. A goal isn't always clearly defined at first. It can be the recognition that you're not happy and that you want to change things in your life so that you'll be happier. A young mother in one of my time management workshops put it this way: "My goal is to have a goal." That is a very legitimate goal.

A man in his early sixties, having taken early retirement from his job, is enjoying the more relaxed pace of retirement, more time to spend with his wife and grown children, and even time to pursue some hobbies. But he feels somehow out of sync—there's something missing in his life. He's a bright, talented guy with financial security and a lot of energy. He wants to fill the gap, but that's as much as he can articulate.

A young woman left her hometown and family after college for a job in recreation in another state. She loves her job, her co-workers, and the children in the programs she supervises, but she too feels an important piece is missing. About all she can put her finger on is that she misses her hometown and her family very much, and she isn't meeting any single people her own age.

At the end of the Introduction I asked you to write down why you decided to read this book, what about you is disorganized, your time problems, etc. Take a moment now to consider some of your goals and write them below. Perhaps you can articulate them as overcoming a problem you identified earlier. If you can, be specific. For example, if you want to get a job with more pay, do you mean you want to double your salary or increase it by 20 percent? If you want to improve your social life, do you mean you want to make a half dozen or so new friends so that you are more likely to have things to do on the weekends? Or, if you want to move to a bigger house, how much bigger, what are you willing to pay—just a ballpark guess—and how soon must you do so? Write down some of your current goals.

Some of My Goals at This Time:

1. _____

2. _____

3. _____

4. _____

5. _____

6. _____

7. _____

8. _____

9. _____

10. _____

Now that you've identified some of your goals, you're ready to get down to bite-size brainstorming.

Compile a List of Bites

The heart of bite-size brainstorming is dividing a goal into individual smaller tasks (or cutting up an elephant into bite-size pieces). You need to focus on the goal you've chosen and then open that mental floodgate and let all your ideas and thoughts about how to accomplish it flow freely.

First you'll need a couple of tools and the right atmosphere. Most of us do our best thinking without outside distractions, so find a quiet, comfortable place where you won't be interrupted—no TV, no phone, no kids. Then pick up a pencil and some paper, focus on your goal, and start writing the bites of your goal—anything and everything that comes to mind when you think about how you could accomplish that goal. Write continuously and don't stop to edit. There are no right or wrong answers, everything is acceptable, and the order of the tasks listed is not important. What you're trying to do is to list *all* the bites.

How long will your list be? That depends on the size of your elephant. How long does bite-size brainstorming take? Usually a few minutes, but again, it depends on the size of your pachyderm.

Here are three of the sample goals, or elephants, listed earlier, with the brainstorming lists compiled by workshop participants.

Make a will.

Call and meet with my lawyer
List my assets
    Real estate
    Equities
    Cash
    Furnishings, etc.
    Insurance
List my concerns
    Guardianships
    Executors
    Joint vs. single ownership
Call and meet with friends
    How have they dealt with similar concerns?

Check library sources
> Book on wills—look for what not to overlook, ways to avoid
>> costly probate, etc.
> Articles—same

Decide to whom I will leave what

Attend public seminars
> Estate planning
> Inheritance tax laws

Change careers

Take courses on changing careers

Talk to friends

Attend job fairs

Read the newspaper

Rewrite my résumé
> Draft a rewrite
> Consult a professional
> Check the library
> Take a course

Check the jobs and careers section at the library

Talk to employment agencies, recruiters, etc.

Write thank you letters after meeting with friends, recruiters,
> etc.

See a career counselor

Make a family Christmas/Hanukkah celebration

Buy gifts
> Plan a budget
> Plan what to buy for whom
> Shop

Make gifts
> Plan a budget
> Plan what to make for whom
> Buy materials
> Make the gifts

Wrap gifts
> Buy paper, ribbon, tape, tags, mailing wrap, labels, etc.
> Wrap
> Hide gifts for the family

Deliver gifts
    Take packages to post office or shipping service
    Call for shipping pickup
    Deliver local gifts
Decorate house
    Buy decorations
    Make decorations
    Put up decorations
Greeting cards
    Make cards
    Buy cards
        Have family photo taken
        Select cards and order printed name
        Family holiday letter
            Write
            Duplicate
    Address envelopes
    Stuff envelopes
    Stamp envelopes
    Mail
Holiday party
    Write guest list
    Invitations
        Buy
        Make
        Write
        Stuff
        Stamp
        Mail
    Write food and beverage menu
    Buy ingredients
    Cook and prepare menu
    Set up for party
    Clean up

Bite-size brainstorming makes a goal less overwhelming, less intimidating. It's just human nature to be more accepting of smaller tasks than larger projects.

A woman I know has a gourmet food shop. The bulk of her business comes from catering parties; few people know her shop is open for lunch, eat-in or take-out. She asked me how to get the word out. I suggested she try bite-size brainstorming. That evening she prepared herself physically—she sat quietly with pencil and paper—and psyched herself mentally—she told herself she didn't have to *do* all of these steps right now. She was merely involved in a fun and creative exercise—making a list. Next she wrote down every idea she could think of for marketing her lunch business. When she felt stuck, she wrote down something preposterous. Her brainstorm list looked like this:

Print flyers about luncheon food and hours to hand to catering customers

Advertise by airplane over town beaches

Have a large "Open for Lunch" sign made for the front window

Advertise on network television

Set up tables and chairs out on the sidewalk

Call two dozen friends and invite them for lunch

Send a press release to the local papers

Next she took each idea, (after editing out airplanes and network TV), and broke it down further to the simplest and smallest tasks she could think of. This whole process took her no more than 15 minutes.

Afterwards my friend told me, "I'm amazed how easy it is and how short my list is. I was overwhelmed by the thought of a 'marketing campaign,' but it looks so much easier when I see it broken down."

One day recently, while serving me and her enthusiastic lunchtime crowd, my catering friend remarked, "Bite-size brainstorming is fun and energizing. I felt terrific because I got started on something I'd been putting off."

This reaction is typical. My workshop participants agree that getting started makes them feel good about themselves. Their lists may not be complete, but that doesn't matter. What matters is that they started—and they're moving. This boosts their morale and provides an added bonus: a burst of energy that they can apply to *doing* the tasks they've listed.

To make sure you understand how to brainstorm, imagine that a friend has asked you to help her get started. Two of her goals are (1) to go back to school for a graduate degree in teaching and (2) to sell her car. List the bites for these elephants below.

Goal 1: Go back to school   **Goal 2: Sell my car**

_____   _____

_____   _____

_____   _____

_____   _____

_____   _____

_____   _____

_____   _____

_____   _____

The purpose of this exercise is to encourage you further to be imaginative, creative, and playful. Sometimes when first introduced to brainstorming my workshop participants find it easier to suggest the bites for someone else's elephant than to make a list for their own goal. Some people feel that asking a friend for a recommendation for, say, a house painter isn't too far removed from asking a friend for suggestions on how to get out word of your restaurant to the lunchtime crowd.

The point is, as with any skill, you'll become more fluent in brainstorming the more you practice.

Now it's your turn. In the pages following, list the bites for three of your own elephants.

Goal 1: _____

_____

_____

_____

_____

_____

_____

_____

_____

_____

_____

_____

_____

_____

_____

_____

_____

_____

_____

_____

_____

_____

_____

_____

Goal 2: _____

_____

_____

_____

_____

_____

_____

_____

_____

_____

_____

_____

_____

_____

_____

_____

_____

_____

_____

_____

_____

_____

_____

_____

_____

_____

_____

_____

Goal 3: _____

_____

_____

_____

_____

_____

_____

_____

_____

_____

_____

_____

_____

_____

_____

_____

_____

_____

_____

_____

_____

_____

_____

_____

_____

_____

_____

Take a look at your lists. If you've listed everything you could think of, undoubtedly you'll be encouraged by what you produced—and by the fact that you've gotten started!

It should be possible to list the bites for any goal, personal or professional. And certainly different people will list different tasks even if their goals are identical. But it's crucial that you get down to the smallest possible bite. Look back at the same brainstorm list for hypothetical goal number 4, change careers. Rewriting one's résumé is one bite of that elephant, but the résumé itself can be broken down into bites, which the brainstormer has done in part. When she reviewed her list, however, she realized that some bites were missing. This is what she finally ended up with under "Rewrite my résumé":

Take a course

Check the library

Consult a professional

Ask my friends

Draft a rewrite

Get some feedback

Type a camera-ready copy

Have it duplicated or printed

Go back and check your bites for your goals 1, 2, and 3. Can you identify any elephants within an elephant? Is each task as small as it can be?

Distinguish Decision Bites from Action Bites

Further refinement of bite-size brainstorming is to identify the *action* bites of an elephant. In brainstorming the "change careers" goal, students new to the brainstorming process frequently offer decision or thinking bites rather than action bites. For example, they might say "First the person dissatisfied with her career must think about what she doesn't like about her job. Then she must think about what she likes to do. Next she must think about what she's good at, what her skills are."

All of these are valid; these decisions do have to be made. But at this rate our poor dissatisfied woman will never get out of her thinking posture and get on with her life. As Andrew Jackson said, "Take time to deliberate; but when the time for action arrives, stop thinking and go in."

Anyone who wants to change careers already has a lot of information about what she doesn't like to do and what she does, and it's only by identifying and performing *actions* that she will achieve her goal and make a change.

Consider the goal of making a will, introduced on page 43. The task of deciding which assets to leave to whom is a major bite of that elephant, and making those decisions is definitely action. But notice that many of the other bites—attend public seminars, call and meet with friends, check library sources—are actions that will get this brainstormer off his duff and moving forward, gathering information so he can make his decisions more quickly.

Many of my workshop students complain they don't make decisions easily. Very often, I've found, that's because they haven't taken the appropriate *actions* to help them gather enough information.

In the exercise below, I have listed some goals followed by a thinking bite. For the first three I've also filled in an action bite. Following those examples, take up your pencil and complete the exercise.

1. Goal: Take up regular exercise.

   Think about: The limitations of my age and health.

   Action: Visit the local YWCA to learn about exercise classes.

2. Goal: Start a small stock portfolio.

   Think about: Do I want income, growth, liquidity . . . ?

   Action: Take a financial planning seminar.

3. Goal: Help families from overseas who move to my community.

   Think about: What would seem most foreign to me if I came to the U.S. from another land?

   Action: Visit my community center to determine which countries most newcomers are emigrating from.

4. Goal: Travel to Europe.

Think about: How little money I have.

Action:_____

5. Goal: Network with other professionals in my field.

Think about: How busy I am and how little time I have.

Action:_____

6. Goal: End an unsatisfying dating relationship.

Think about: How I'm going to tell him.

Action:_____

7. Goal: Change a zoning regulation in my town.

Think about: What a long, uphill battle it will be.

Action:_____

8. Goal: To expand my "picky eater" daughter's food repertoire.

Think about: All the foods she hates.

Action:_____

9. Goal: To spend more quality time with my spouse.

Think about: Where I can cut other commitments.

Action:_____

10. Goal: To improve conditions for the homeless in my city.

Think about: The enormity of the task and my limited resources.

Action:_____

Notice that the "thoughts" in examples 1, 4, 5, 6, 7, 8, and 10 are all negative. Many people never get started in what they want to do because they feel immobilized by negative thoughts. This exercise is always an eye-opener in my workshops. It demonstrates that for every negative (or positive) thought, there are positive, get-you-going actions.

Now go back to the exercise in which you brainstormed the bites for three of your goals. Have you listed thinking bites or action bites? Mark each task with an A for action or a T for thinking. Where you identified a thinking task, can it be translated into an appropriate action? If so, write the action beside it.

When discussing decision versus action, it's important not to split hairs. Many goals entail creative thinking tasks. From composing a jingle to plotting a prosecution, from writing a slogan to outlining a program of medical treatment, from designing a logo to planning a family's menu, thought is the germ of creation. It's just that you must not stop with thinking but must carry the thought through by doing.

Classify the Action Bites

When you look at several brainstorming lists side by side, you'll notice certain tasks appear regularly, such as "take a workshop, seminar, or class"; "talk to my friends"; and "go to the library." Translated, these bites represent education, communication, and research, which are the cornerstones of problem solving. You will find these bites on many of your brainstorming lists.

This is a technique to help you get started, a way to orient yourself mentally. If you start to bite-size brainstorm but the blank page keeps staring back at you, you can ask yourself, "Do I need to educate myself?" (Take a course or consult an expert.) "Will I help to accomplish my goal by telling my friends what I'm trying to do?" (Communicate.) "Can I find information at the library or other community resource?" (Research.)

If the communications department introduced at the beginning of the chapter had talked ("Communication") regularly to upper management, they could have avoided producing inaccurate and unusable brochures. If the young physician had read up ("Research") on dogs, their needs and idiosyncracies, he might have avoided the costly damage to his furnishings.

How to Open a Rusty Floodgate

If you have trouble getting started on bite-size brainstorming—you have pencil in hand, but the ideas, or bites, just don't flow—here are several unblocking techniques used by writers that you can apply to bite-size brainstorming (or, for that matter, to starting anything).

Write a Letter to a Friend

Take some of the pressure off yourself and explain to a friend what you're trying to do. "Dear Mary," you might write, "I have to clean out the attic—it's reached fire hazard status!—and I'm having trouble getting started. I'm supposed to break down the project into small tasks, and all I can think of is going up into the attic, taking a look at the horrible scene, coming back down, and putting it off for another year. The job seems so big and overwhelming! Help!

"One thing I know for sure: at least half of what's up there can be thrown out . . . thrown out . . . well, I guess I'll need some garbage bags and plenty of twist-ties. But what if I find things I don't need anymore but are too good to be thrown out? I could take them to the thrift shop or Goodwill. Then I'd better assemble some empty cartons . . . that means a trip to the shopping center for some boxes. But most of what's in the attic is pure junk . . . it'll be too much for the garbage collector, though. I'd better arrange for a dump run. Now, how do I find someone to do that? I know, I'll call Elizabeth. She had someone haul her stuff away after her yard sale.

"But, Mary, I don't want to throw everything away. I need to save some of what's in the attic. How do I arrange everything so I can find it when I need to? More cartons . . . and markers for writing on them. . . ."

You don't have to read more of this woman's letter to Mary to realize that the letter is the brainstorm. Garbage bags, twist-ties, cartons, thrift shop, dump run, and markers are some of the bites to her elephant. Sitting down with a scratch pad and pencil—again, nothing is carved in stone here—and writing a letter to a friend is a very effective way to begin brainstorming when you're having a hard time getting started, or thinking of the bites.

The letter-to-a-friend example points out one of the biggest benefits of bite-size brainstorming: it gives you a chance to think of the *equipment* you'll need to accomplish your goal. The bites of the "clean out my attic" elephant include garbage bags, twist-ties, cartons, and markers. If the well-intentioned but ill-prepared high school students from the beginning of the chapter had bite-size brainstormed before the car wash, they might have recognized as necessary a reliable water source and publicity posters.

Not having the necessary equipment is an obstacle to accomplishing any goal. Furthermore, habitual procrastinators often use the excuse of out-of-stock tools for not getting started on their tasks.

No one can deny that the most important bite of the goal "clean the attic" is to *clean the attic*. The final task is still at hand after all the brainstorming, planning, and preparation have been done. However, if it's a large space, the woman can break it up into four corners, so many shelves, so many racks of clothes, so many cartons, or whatever is feasible.

Keep Your Pencil on the Paper

Sometimes your brainstorming stumbling block might not be getting started but *continuing*. You've listed a few bites, but they're still so large that you don't know where to go next.

No matter what, keep writing and don't stop to edit. Make your grocery list if you have to; list the days of the week; do whatever it takes to keep your pencil moving. If you can't think of a friend or relative to write to, you can try beginning with "I have to do this brainstorm, and I can't think of what to write, but it's about. . . ."

Remember the two suggestions presented earlier: 1) focus on communication, education, and research, and 2) think of actions as well as thoughts.

Use a Tape Recorder

Some people are threatened by writing but are very comfortable talking. You can speak your brainstorm into a tape recorder, play it back, and transcribe it. This unblocking device, frequently used by professional writers, can help you get started on a project if you insist your ideas flow better through your mouth than through your fingertips.

Ask a Friend to Help

Brainstorming with a friend is a surefire way to accomplish this step. If you're having trouble thinking of the bites to your elephant or applying the seat of your pants to the seat of the chair, there's nothing like the support, encouragement, and ideas of a family member, close friend, or business colleague.

Check for Physical Stumbling Blocks

The suggestions above help to take the onus away from "I." And what's wrong with asking for a little help? Review your brainstorming environment; perhaps external, rather than mental, factors are putting up barriers. Have you assembled the necessary brainstorming tools—pencil and paper; tape recorder, batteries, and blank tape; or a friend? Have you removed yourself from distractions and protected yourself from interruptions?

It's easy to fall into the trap of not being prepared to do something and therefore give yourself a reason not to do it: "Oh, I can't clean out the attic, because I haven't gathered any empty cartons." To repeat, lack of the necessary materials gives us further fuel to procrastinate.

The same can be said for distractions and interruptions. If the rabble of four boisterous children indoors on a rainy day is distracting you from completing a brainstorming exercise, you must remove either yourself from their noise or them from your immediate environment.

"It's the constant distractions and interruptions that keep me from tackling my goals," complained the single mother of two small children who attended a workshop. "How can I find quiet time for myself?" she asked.

That was her elephant. The workshop participants suggested:

1. Stay up after your kids go to sleep.
2. Get up in the morning before your kids wake up.
3. Get a sitter and go to your branch library.
4. Drop off your kids at a friend's or relative's and drive your car to a park.

Whether you're a Fortune 500 company determined to double profits in five years or a homemaker intent upon a tidy attic, the process of accomplishing that goal begins with brainstorming. And brainstorming consists of the bites of assembling the tools, finding a quiet place, and blocking out some quiet time.

On Day Two you should brainstorm a list of tasks for everything you want to do, each goal on a separate piece of paper.

True, you seldom encounter one elephant at a time. In your busy life you often come face to face with a stampede of elephants. One of my workshop participants laughingly recalled, "A therapist friend told us never to undertake too many major life changes at once, but my husband changed jobs, we moved, and I had a baby, all in the same year."

The first step to getting through the stampede, in an organized way, is to list the bites of one elephant, then another, then another.

And don't forget the lesson from Day One: when you complete this part of the process, give yourself a big reward for a job well done.

DAY 2

1. Identify your goals (elephants).

2. Assemble your bite-size brainstorming tools and find an environment free of distractions and interruptions.

3. List the bites (steps) to accomplishing each goal on a separate piece of paper.

4. Ask yourself, "Do I need to communicate with anyone, educate myself, or research the topic?"

5. Check each list to make sure all the bites are as small as possible.

6. Make sure your lists contain action bites, as well as thinking bites.

Give yourself a reward!

DAY

3

The Pocket
Notebook and
Other Papers

By now you have lists of rewards from Day One and brainstorming lists for your goals from Day Two. What's to be done with all these bites, or tasks? On Day Three you'll learn how to organize all the bites of your elephants.

Go back for a moment to the fantasy world with unlimited time mentioned in the Preface. If you lived in such a world, you would eat one elephant at a time. You would accomplish each goal, from first task to last, without interruption from any other goals. If you set about changing careers, for example, you would do all the tasks on your brainstorm list, one by one, until you had a new job. Then you might tackle your next elephant, perhaps finding a new apartment or finding a spouse.

My personal philosophy echoes Thoreau, who said, "Simplify, simplify." I'm all in favor of not overcrowding my life by taking on more elephants than I can manage, but the tunnel-vision concept of eating one elephant at a time is totally unrealistic in the world of 24 hours a day and the many deadlines within those hours. Since I must write (this book, for example), work at a part-time job, do volunteer work in my community, and last but *not* least, be a wife and mother, I have to manage all these demands at the same time. The way I manage them, and save time, is to group similar tasks together.

Divide Your Tasks into Four Categories

All of the bites to my elephants are either phone calls, errands, things to do, or things to write. These are the only categories of tasks that exist. Similarly, all of the bites on your brainstorming lists are either phone calls, errands, things to do, or things to write. Go back and look at your brainstorm lists from Day Two. Can you find any task that doesn't fit one of the four categories? The "do" category is indeed a catchall. If a task is not a call, an errand, or something to write, then it's something to do.

Communication bites of your elephant are usually phone calls to speak to people, errands to meet with them, or letters to write to them. Education bites might be calls to ask questions of experts or consultants or an errand to sign up for a course. And research bites might be an errand to the library or some reading to do. Remember, focusing on communication, education, and research is a way to orient your thinking for bite-size brainstorming. Calls, errands, things to do, and things to write are the categories of bites you come up with.

Most people already habitually group together things that are alike. You put coats in a coat closet, laundry in the laundry basket, and tools in the toolbox, and you keep a running list of what you need at the grocery store, that is, items that can all be found at one store. One reason for grouping tasks together is to accomplish them more quickly. When you have several phone calls to make, for example, you set aside 15 minutes to make phone calls, one after the other. Likewise, when you're going out in your car, you do several errands on one trip from home. People call meetings to discuss several issues at one sitting. Grouping like tasks together is more effective than making one call, doing one errand, and then moving to the typewriter to write a memo, only to go back out and do more errands. Furthermore, by doing several similar tasks, one after the other, you create a rhythm and a sense of momentum, as well as a greater feeling of accomplishment.

The second reason for grouping similar bites together is to be better able to look over the group and decide what you want to do first. (Setting priorities is discussed in detail in Day Five.)

Using two of the sample goals and their brainstorming lists from Day Two, here are examples of dividing tasks into the four categories. Starting with the "Change Careers" goal, the bites are classified as follows:

Change Careers

Calls

- ☐ re courses
- ☐ friends in other fields
- ☐ career counselor(s)
- ☐ employment agencies and recruiters

Errands

- ☐ register and take course(s)
- ☐ meet with friends in other fields
- ☐ meet with career counselor
- ☐ check the career section at the library
- ☐ visit employment agencies and recruiters
- ☐ have new résumé printed

Do

- ☐ read newspaper ads

Write

- ☐ outline new résumé
- ☐ draft new résumé
- ☐ write final résumé
- ☐ write thank you letters to friends, etc.

Keep in mind that the tasks in the lists above are sometimes too general. Under phone calls, your tasks should apply specifically to you. For example, one individual might write:

- ☐ Call Jerry to meet and talk about public relations.
- ☐ Call Samantha to meet and talk about investor relations.
- ☐ Call Carol to meet and talk about media buying.
- ☐ Call Ted to meet and talk about advertising.

Obviously this person is interested in the communications field and has thought of friends and acquaintances from whom she can gather information and ask advice.

As you know, in real life you have to manage several elephants at the same time. If two of your goals were to change careers and make a will, adding the tasks for the latter would produce task lists that look like this:

Calls

- ☐ re courses
- ☐ friends in other fields
- ☐ career counselor(s)
- ☐ employment agencies and recruiters
- ☐ my lawyer
- ☐ friends about their wills
- ☐ re seminars on wills

Errands

- ☐ register and take course(s)
- ☐ meet with friends in other fields
- ☐ meet with career counselor
- ☐ check the career section at the library
- ☐ visit employment agencies and recruiters
- ☐ have new résumé printed
- ☐ meet with lawyer
- ☐ meet with friends re wills
- ☐ check library re wills
- ☐ attend seminars re wills

Do

- ☐ read newspaper ads
- ☐ list my assets
- ☐ list my concerns re will
- ☐ decide to whom I will leave what

Write

- ☐ outline new résumé
- ☐ draft new résumé
- ☐ write final résumé
- ☐ write thank you letters to friends, etc.

Now it's your turn. Taking all the brainstorms you did in the preceding chapter, organize all the bites into the four categories on the pages that follow.

Calls

_____

_____

_____

_____

_____

_____

_____

_____

_____

_____

_____

_____

_____

_____

_____

_____

_____

_____

_____

_____

_____

_____

_____

_____

_____

_____

_____

_____

_____

_____

_____

Errands

_____
_____
_____
_____
_____
_____
_____
_____
_____
_____
_____
_____
_____
_____
_____
_____
_____
_____
_____
_____
_____
_____
_____
_____
_____
_____
_____
_____
_____
_____
_____
_____

Do

Write

_____
_____
_____
_____
_____
_____
_____
_____
_____
_____
_____
_____
_____
_____
_____
_____
_____
_____
_____
_____
_____
_____
_____
_____
_____
_____
_____
_____

When you've completed this exercise, what you have in front of you is your entire task list, everything you have to or want to do for all of your goals. (This is different from a daily "to do" list, which is much shorter and is the subject of Day Five.)

Buy a Pocket Notebook

You now have lists of calls, errands, things to do, and things to write. That's fine, but you have limited space in this book. To continue the process and keep yourself organized for life, I recommend that when you've finished this book you purchase a pocket notebook, a small notebook that goes with you everywhere, and transfer your call, errand, do, and write lists to that. Some people prefer a spiral notebook, others choose a loose-leaf style. Still others select one of the many personal planners on the market today. It doesn't matter which you choose. What does matter is that you have it with you at all times so you can write in it whenever you think of something you want to do.

Many people who take my workshops insist that they write everything down, but they write on whatever scrap of paper happens to be handy—memo pads, legal pads, paper napkins, even matchbook covers. Committing their thoughts to paper is a good intention, but doing so in many different places is very risky.

Once I attended a meeting of volunteers for a community arts organization. While the president of the group was making notes on our thoughts and decisions, there was much spreading out and shuffling of papers—budgets to review, artwork to consider, and so on. Halfway through the meeting I realized the president was making notes in many places. Several days later I wasn't a bit surprised when she telephoned to say she'd misplaced an important number, scribbled on the back of one of her many slips of paper.

Many workshop participants confess they write lists and then lose them. The very obvious, and timesaving, cure is to keep all the lists in one place, your pocket notebook.

Keep Track of Everything That's Important to You

Now you have a small notebook that contains four lists. What about all the other blank pages? What are they used for? You can use them to record anything else you'd like to keep track of, anything that pertains to your life.

Sarah M., the computer programmer introduced in Day One, keeps a list of baby-sitters' names and phone numbers and also a list of books recommended by friends that she wants to check out from her library. Bank president Donald R. keeps track of everything from agenda items for the next board of directors meeting to vacation ideas for him and his wife. And Peter R., the construction foreman, writes on one page everything he needs to tell his boss. On another he writes what he wants to remember to tell his brother when he calls him long-distance. On still another he writes gift ideas for his favorite nephew.

What about rewards? Yes, they definitely belong in your notebook. One homemaker who took my workshop complained bitterly that upon receiving an unexpected gift of time—her mother stopped by unannounced to watch her three small children for two hours—she didn't have a clue as to how she wanted to enjoy herself. "The opportunity for a little self-indulgence caught me completely unprepared," she said. "I spent the time doing boring little errands, errands I could have easily done while accompanied by my children." Too late she recalled that little shop in the next town that she had passed and wanted to go back to. Too late she remembered her friend's photography exhibit at her branch library.

I know a successful salesperson for a greeting card and paper-ware company who keeps a page in her notebook for each of the clients she calls on. When she thinks of particular merchandise for a certain client, she writes it on that client's page. When she needs to bring up a matter of an overdue bill, she makes a note on the client's page, and when she wants to congratulate a client on the birth of his first grandchild, she makes a note of that as well. Keeping her thoughts on each client together has brought my friend bigger accounts and an expanding client group. And this is as simple as writing something down in the appropriate place when you think of it.

Here are more examples of pocket notebook page headings, culled from participants in my workshops:

☐ Order from office supply store
☐ Country inns I want to try
☐ Clothing needs for Alexis (same for Susan and Jim)
☐ Questions for builder
☐ Remember to take to Maine
☐ Manhattan sights for kids

❑ Books I want to read
❑ Questions for my lawyer
❑ Videotapes I want to see
❑ Gift ideas for Mom
❑ Agenda for next staff meeting
❑ Look up at the library
❑ Wish list
❑ Questions for software store

One workshop student suggested, "My pocket notebook is really like a mini–filing cabinet," which is a very good description.

In the space below, write down other timesaving lists you might keep in your pocket notebook. Think of people you regularly talk to on the phone or correspond with. Do you need to keep track of what to tell them? Do you ever hear yourself saying "I know there's something else I want to mention, but I can't remember what?" Forgetting is hardly a serious offense, and everyone does it at one time or another, but it wastes time—time you could be spending having fun.

Additional Page Titles for My Pocket Notebook

1. _____
2. _____
3. _____
4. _____
5. _____
6. _____
7. _____
8. _____
9. _____
10. _____
11. _____
12. _____

The List as a Usable Tool

It's important to keep in mind that lists are tools — tools to help you become and stay organized and save time. They should not be a compulsion.

In the past, list makers have earned a bad reputation. There's an image of a nervous, skinny little guy in a corner, endlessly making lists. He writes furiously and compulsively, and needless to say, he never gets around to doing any of the tasks on his lists. He's too busy writing.

I have a friend who writes her lists in different-colored felt-tip markers. Her penmanship resembles calligraphy, and she even embellishes her lists with flowers, rainbows, butterflies, and so on. Her lists are artwork, not tools. Is it any wonder she often complains about not accomplishing anything?

Use Your Notebook as a Memory File

ORGANIZATIONAL MYTH NO. 6: *"I can remember everything."*

This is indeed a myth, put forth by the "increase your memory" folks making their way around the lecture and training circuits these days. I do accept that you can learn to improve your memory, but increased skill in that area will never replace the need to write things down.

I once attended one of these memory-enhancing sessions. The expert demonstrated how to memorize the colonial states in the order in which they ratified the Constitution. The process involved inventing an outrageous visual image, one state piled upon another. All that I retained is that Connecticut was the first state to ratify the Constitution, and I'm not sure I can attribute that to the mnemonic device—was it simply that I live in Connecticut and all license plates here read "Constitution State"? No matter. I left this workshop with the same conviction with which I entered: that I should write down anything I need to remember. This way I'm open to inspiration. I free my brain from the job of remembering so I can be creative.

This brings me to another definition of a brainstorm, "a flash of insight." My pocket notebook is a place to keep the bites of my elephants, but it's also where I write down any idea that comes to mind that is worth saving.

When I thought of an example to include in this book while cooking breakfast, I jotted it down in my notebook. When I'm relaxing with the newspaper and a mug of tea, and I think of someone I want to get to know better, someone I want to have lunch with, I write it in my notebook. And yes, when I'm driving my car and I pass a store or a point of interest I'd like to return to, I pull off the road and make a note of it.

Have you ever been in a social situation, where the conversation has not been about work or professions or what people do for a living, when suddenly a man pulls a small notebook out of his breast pocket and writes something down? I've often observed very successful men and women do this—at black-tie dinners and tennis matches, at theatrical openings and on the beach. Making a note of something you want to remember takes less than 30 seconds, and I've never seen the writer's company offended. On the contrary, they're usually impressed.

On the other hand, I've often attended meetings where nothing is written down. Perhaps a leader is delegating responsibilities for work to be done. I've seen subordinates nod and say, "Sure, I'll take care of it," but they don't write anything down. How are they going to remember? Very often they don't.

As Lee Iacocca wrote in his autobiography, "The discipline of writing something down is the first step to making it happen." Successful people everywhere, as well as the organizing experts, agree: you're more likely to get things done, to move ahead, to realize your goals if you write things down. Memory gurus are so busy remembering that they have much less time for doing.

An interesting side benefit also accrues when you cultivate the habit of writing things down: more and more ideas come to mind. You find yourself thinking creatively and coming up with practical solutions for your problems with a minimum of agonizing worry.

One week after starting to keep a pocket notebook, a young woman told me she had thought of six ideas for home-based businesses she wanted to start. We both agreed she should try one before beginning another, but she kept her brain tuned to the search for viable business ideas, which she recorded on a page in her notebook.

The young woman discovered that once she started writing down ideas, she became alert to other ideas. Her antennae were up and she started to make new connections and associations. Her ideas weren't goals yet; she was merely trying them on like so many pairs of shoes. Once she found an idea for a business that fit her needs, interests, lifestyle, and so on, she would begin a bite-size brainstorm. Until then, the page in her pocket notebook was simply a place to store her creative ideas for safe keeping.

A man and wife were very concerned about the buildup of nuclear arms among the superpowers and wanted to do something toward arms reduction, but they confessed that they felt a little like two ants trying to push a boulder up a mountain. After they began writing down ideas related to their respective jobs, they found that the habit, and the resulting flow of ideas, carried over into their after-work lives. Today they are actively involved in their community's nuclear freeze movement, which is making headlines in the press as well as influencing their elected officials.

Again, the couple didn't define their goal as "end the buildup of nuclear arms." Instead, they opened their minds to smaller goals that they could realistically accomplish. After adding to and refining the pages of their pocket notebooks entitled "Nuclear Freeze" for several weeks, they chose to hold a demonstration followed by a press conference.

You may have noticed in Day Two that often the most profound insights come after you've completed the initial bite-size brainstorm of your elephant. Any brainstorming session should have a beginning and an end, whether you spend five minutes or an hour breaking down your goal into manageable tasks. When you stop, you may have stopped your car, so to speak, but the motor is still idling. Even though you may move to do something totally unrelated to that elephant, your subconscious is still percolating. Suddenly, like a bolt of lightning, you get an idea. What should you do? Stop what you're doing just long enough to write it down in your pocket notebook. I can attest to the fact that, though brainstorming produces viable solutions, letting the problem simmer for a couple days often makes even more solutions come to mind.

Unfortunately, there are no "lost and found" tables for lost ideas. When an idea bubbles to the surface, like a fragile bubble on water, it can be lost forever in an instant.

At this point in my workshops, students often ask "How much time do you spend writing every day?" With rare exception, I spend less than five minutes a day doing brainstorms or recording ideas in my pocket notebook. (Perhaps once or twice a week I brainstorm elephants that require 30 minutes or more to identify the smaller tasks.) It's a habit I maintain so I can stay organized, but as a total amount of time spent, it's very small. I spend most of my time doing work that I enjoy and having fun.

Take Control of Paper

Now you have a pocket notebook to keep track of all the bites of all of your elephants, to list other matters that routinely come up, and to remind you of any ideas on any subject that may have come to mind. It's all very neat and tidy, but what about that mountain of paper on your home or office desk?

Managing paper flow is also a large part of what I do every day. It's a big part of any organizing process, and indeed entire books have been written on this subject alone. But all the experts concur: there are just three things you can do with a piece of paper—throw it out, file it, or act on it. Most people don't do enough of the first, they do too much of the second, and the third almost always gets them into trouble.

Go back for a moment to the fantasy world of unlimited time. If you recall, a businessperson would typically sit at his desk, go through his "in" box, and act on each piece of paper through its completion. Likewise, a retired person at home would bring in the mail and act on each piece in turn. If she has received a piece of "junk" mail, she pitches it into the wastebasket. If the next piece is a subscription magazine, she sits down and reads it. If the next envelope is a letter from her daughter, she reads it and then answers it. And so on.

As you know, the real world imposes many deadlines, and most people are forced to act on the paper they receive. Bills are due by a certain date, your daughter's school requests a medical form before she can begin the fall term, most states require that you renew your automobile registration, etc.—the paper molehill can quickly grow to mountainous proportions. What's the most effective and timesaving way to process all the paper that rains on you every day?

ORGANIZATIONAL MYTH No. 7: *"I should handle a piece of paper only once."*

This myth is quoted often by people who think they know how to manage paper effectively. The truth is most people who are organized handle paper *two* times, first to sort it into tasks and second to act on it.

Sort Your Mail

For mail at home, I recommend the following sorting process:

1. Throw away the junk.
2. Place bills to be paid in a "bills" or "financial" file, which you pull out once or twice a month.
3. Set aside material you want to read.
4. File anything you must save.
5. Put papers requiring an action into a file called "pending."

The papers that require action translate into calls, errands, things to do, and things to write, and as such they should be entered in your pocket notebook. For example:

☐ Postcard from your dentist reminding you it's time for a checkup **(call)**

☐ Advertisement from a department store (**errand**—the store is having a sale on televisions, and you need a new one)

☐ An invitation to a party (**call** to reply yes or no)

☐ Your community center bulletin says the center is sponsoring a clothing drive (**do**—collect what your kids have outgrown)

☐ An agenda for your co-op's residents' meeting (**write** up summary of estimates from security companies for installation of surveillance cameras in lobby, elevators, etc.)

☐ A bill for X rays following an automobile accident (**do**—complete and send insurance form)

☐ A letter from a friend **(write)**

Mail at work is processed similarly. Very often the papers that senior executives find in their "in" boxes have been presorted according to urgency by an assistant. Nevertheless, all of us, from secretaries to CEOs, must look at our pieces of paper, first to identify the kind of task each represents and second to act on them.

In the space below, list what you found in your mail today, either at home or at work. Beside its number, write the action you assigned to it.

Action Tasks from Mail

_____	1. _____
_____	2. _____
_____	3. _____
_____	4. _____
_____	5. _____
_____	6. _____
_____	7. _____
_____	8. _____
_____	9. _____
_____	10. _____
_____	11. _____
_____	12. _____
_____	13. _____
_____	14. _____
_____	15. _____
_____	16. _____
_____	17. _____
_____	18. _____
_____	19. _____
_____	20. _____

When my workshop participants complain that their desks are piled high with papers, I explain that the way to begin is to sort through the piles and to write the appropriate tasks in their notebooks. Then they're ready to act on the papers in their pending files. Why not just start acting on each piece as you come across it? As I said at the beginning of the chapter, you must organize the tasks so you can look them all over and determine which are most important. (You'll come to setting priorities in Day Five.)

Be Realistic About How Much You Can Read

A word about what you want to, or have to, read. People who've taken my workshops have confessed to hoarding mountains of good intentions—newspapers, periodicals, books, and now the prolific mail-order catalogues that they're going to read "someday." I've seen large sofas covered with reading material and entire rooms piled high with newsletters, journals, magazines, newspapers, press kits, manuscripts, file folders—in short, an atomic explosion of paper.

When I first became involved in the writing business, a magazine editor made me understand this quote from the Bible: "There is no new thing under the sun." He told me, "Every article that you're going to read or write has been written before and will be written again." Topics often recur every two years in magazines, he went on to explain, certainly much more often in the daily media. And he took his hat off to the dozens of women's magazines that month after month contain still one more diet article, reworked, reslanted, repackaged, but all of which can be reduced to what everyone already knows: eat less and exercise more.

As a result of this insight, I forgive myself much more readily when I don't have time to read something. "Oh, what the heck, it'll be back again in two years," I say as I bundle another pile of papers for the recycling bin.

Many people must read to stay current in their field, and most of us also read for pleasure. As a consultant in time management and organization, I try to read all the books and articles concerning the topic. As a writer, I try always to read good writing. Likewise, my friends in the financial world read the financial press. My friends in the hotel and restaurant business read their trade publications, and the teachers, physicians, and salespeople I know read about the latest developments in their professions. However, those who keep from drowning in a sea of reading matter have realistic expectations for just how much they can read. They don't subscribe to more than they can make time for.

The students in my workshops have consistently agreed: piles of unread material are depressing. They deflate your morale by reminding you of unaccomplished goals. Students who develop realistic expectations for how much they can read designate a small space for this material—one shelf, one table top, one pile on the credenza, or whatever else works. As the pile exceeds its boundaries, they throw away what they know they're not going to get around to reading. It's important to remember that, just as you'll never get everything done, you'll never get everything read.

ORGANIZATIONAL MYTH NO. 8: *"If I think I'll need it, I should file it."*

Recently I heard a frightening statistic: 80 percent of what people file they never retrieve. A colleague who also heard this remark, and who considers himself one who saves very little paper, went home and riffled through his files, only to realize that he, too, seldom retrieves anything from them. And he spends many hours every two years weeding out the "dead wood," that is, what he no longer deems worth keeping.

Set Up a "Halfway House" for Paper

When you're handling a piece of paper and trying to decide whether or not you should save it, don't ask, "Is there a chance I might need this?" Ask instead, "If I need this later, do I know where, or from whom, I can get it quickly?" If the answer is yes, throw yours out!

This is especially good advice in the workplace where many people receive duplicates of letters, memos, reports and what have you. For your personal files at home, consult your accountant or attorney if you're not sure what to save.

Many people in my workshops agonize over what to save and what to toss. For these students I recommend using what I call a "halfway house." This is typically a box of papers and other items placed "out of sight, out of mind" and dated a year or two hence.

Even though she had settled her husband's estate, a widow I knew was afraid to throw away any piece of paper relating to his affairs. And yet being surrounded by all this paper, little of which she understood without her attorney, was weighing her down emotionally. She needed to put it behind her and get on with the next phase of her life. For her, a halfway house was the answer. She bundled up everything her attorney told her she did not need to save, put it in a carton, labeled its contents, dated it for two years hence, and stored it in a corner of her basement. As her attorney predicted, she had no occasion to unearth her papers, and out they went with the trash on the appointed date.

A similar story was told to me by a man who assumed the post of commodore for a small boat club in a summer community in Michigan. He set about organizing many old photos, scrapbooks, minutes from meetings, and the like, but saw no purpose in keeping many pieces that were undated or unidentified. Rather than just dump everything, he designed a section of the boat club's loft to house several cartons of this miscellany in case anyone should come forward to look for or claim something. Not surprisingly, the boxes remained undisturbed until their appointed date with the garbage truck.

After you have read, understood, and completed the exercises in this chapter, check your task lists: is one item on your errand list to purchase a pocket notebook? Good work! Give yourself a big reward.

DAY 3

☑ ☑ ☑ ☐ ☐

1. Divide your tasks into calls, errands, things to do, and things to write.

2. Transfer your tasks to a pocket notebook.

3. Use the extra pages for other routine lists.

4. Jot down all your ideas as reminders.

Other Paper

1. Sort your mail with an eye to tasks.

2. Throw away reading material you won't have time for.

3. Set a "discard" deadline for all questionable paper.

Give yourself a reward!

The Pocket
Calendar

This book is becoming filled with dozens of calls, errands, things to do, and things to write. Now what do you do? How do you get from organized tasks to decisive action? Implementation doesn't just happen. Each bite takes a finite amount of time to accomplish. You'll need a calendar for implementing your bites, since you have to plug them into times in your life.

Day Four is devoted to the effective use of calendars. Almost everyone uses calendars these days—wall calendars, desk blotter calendars, digital calendars, even computer calendars. Like lists, calendars are tools. Depending on how you use them, they can help you get organized, remember things, and plan, and thus save time, or they can be time-wasters if you fail to carry them with you, if you fail to write on them, if you fail to read what you wrote, or if you fail to transfer bites onto them. Let's look at how to get the most benefit from your calendar.

List Your External Appointments

Most people record appointments with other people—what the experts call "external" appointments—on their calendars. They write down meetings with lawyers, doctors, the PTA, the car mechanic, and so on. For example, Jim R. owns a delivery service business. His calendar might look like this:

> *Tuesday*
>
> Susan and Luke's anniversary
>
> 7:30 A.M.   Breakfast meeting with Ted
>
> 9:30 A.M.   Staff meeting
>
> 1:30 P.M.   Meet with purchasing
>
> 8:00 P.M.   "Go to School" night

What is on your calendar for tomorrow? In the space below, write down your external appointments.

Tomorrow's Date _____

Time   *Appointment*

_____   _____

_____   _____

_____   _____

_____   _____

_____   _____

_____   _____

Calendars are often vastly underused. They can also serve to remind you of "internal" appointments, that is, the deadlines you set for yourself but for which no one says "It must be done today." Tasks from your pocket notebook such as drafting a new résumé, writing a letter to the editor at the local newspaper about an issue that concerns you, tracking down that artist whose work you admired at the sidewalk art show, and visiting a travel agent to discuss vacation ideas don't usually have deadlines attached to them.

What are some bites for your elephants for which you have not yet assigned a deadline? Write several below.

_____

_____

_____

_____

_____

_____

_____

Sometimes we procrastinate because the elephant is too big. The solution, of course, is to break it down into the smallest bites. Other times we procrastinate because our tasks are disorganized. The solution: to organize them in a pocket notebook. Still other times we procrastinate because we haven't made an appointment with ourselves to get a task done. People put off doing all kinds of tasks, but it's the jobs that don't have a deadline that we procrastinate about most often.

Add Internal Appointments

By identifying a block of time on your calendar and writing in the job to be done, you go a long way toward accomplishing the task. Writing it down doesn't ensure that you'll do it, but it brings you much closer than just thinking about doing it.

Here is Jim R.'s calendar with internal appointments included.

Tuesday

Susan and Luke's anniversary

7:30 A.M.	Breakfast meeting with Ted
9:30 A.M.	Staff meeting
10:45 A.M.	Draft new marketing strategy
1:30 P.M.	Meet with purchasing
2:30 P.M.	Review personnel policies handbook
8:00 P.M.	"Go to School" night

Jim's vice president wrote a proposal for a new delivery service he wants to begin offering, but before he and Jim sit down with their advertising agency Jim wants to gather his thoughts about how the service ought to be marketed ("draft new marketing strategy"). Second, the personnel policies for his company were compiled into a pamphlet five years ago, but the manual is now hopelessly out of date and needs to be redone ("review personnel policies handbook"). Jim's company can't establish a delivery service until a marketing strategy is done, and the firm's lawyer has repeatedly urged Jim to get going on the personnel handbook, especially in light of recent employment legislation. Somehow, however, both tasks always get put on the back burner, so "draft new marketing strategy" and "review personnel policies handbook" are tasks that regularly appear in Jim's pocket notebook—and just sit there. After learning the importance of setting deadlines for such postponed tasks and writing these internal appointments in his calendar, Jim finds that most of the time he gets jobs like these done.

Look at your calendar for tomorrow. Can you find time for some internal appointments? Add them below.

Tomorrow's Date _____

Time   *Appointment*

_____   _____

_____   _____

_____   _____

_____   _____

_____   _____

_____   _____

_____   _____

_____   _____

_____   _____

_____   _____

_____   _____

Setting Up Rewards

The only things missing from your calendar now are rewards. There's no need to write down every coffee break, but you should definitely include larger rewards. (Remember, the reason you write something down—a task in your notebook, an appointment on your calendar, a reward—is to remember it. It's not necessary, and certainly not time-saving, to write down what's obvious or automatic.) Having lunch with a friend, playing squash after work, getting a manicure, and window-shopping are examples of rewards you might write on your calendar.

Look at Jim R.'s calendar now that he has included rewards.

Tuesday

Susan and Luke's anniversary

7:30 A.M.	Breakfast meeting with Ted
9:30 A.M.	Staff meeting
10:45 A.M.	Draft new marketing strategy
12:30 P.M.	Lunch in the park
1:30 P.M.	Meet with purchasing
2:30 P.M.	Review personnel policies handbook
6:30 P.M.	Dinner with my wife
8:00 P.M.	"Go to School" night

Notice that Jim has learned how to use rewards correctly. He inserts them into his day after he meets an internal deadline. When Jim looks at his calendar, the planned reward he sees there is often an incentive for him to get started on the task at hand.

Jim's internal appointments and his rewards for meeting them are, of course, not carved in stone. "Lunch in the park" could get preempted by something unexpected that demands immediate attention. Jim's plan to spend time on the new marketing strategy could be postponed if something more urgent comes up in the staff meeting. (However, by writing them down on his calendar, he has identified free time in his day for both internal tasks and rewards, and making an appointment for them brings Jim much closer to accomplishing his goals.)

In the space below, complete your calendar for tomorrow, including rewards.

Tomorrow's Date _____

Time	Appointment
_____	_____
_____	_____
_____	_____
_____	_____
_____	_____
_____	_____
_____	_____
_____	_____
_____	_____
_____	_____
_____	_____

Keep Your Pocket Calendar With You

As on Day Three, where I urged you to keep a pocket notebook with you at all times, on Day Four I recommend that you take a pocket calendar with you wherever you go. Why? It saves time.

I've met many people who use calendars very conscientiously, but they never have them with them. When the date for the next meeting is being set, they don't know if they're free because their calendar is on their desk. When a customer asks when next week the product representative can return, the rep says, "My calendar's on my desk at the office. I'll have to call you." And when a friend stops you in the aisle of the grocery store and asks if you can come for dinner on Saturday night, you reply that you'll have to go home and check your calendar on the refrigerator door. Filling out a calendar and then not keeping it at hand is simply a time-waster. Not having your calendar within reach whenever you need it means you have to remember to call the person back and then find the time to do so—which, in turn, means another call to add to your pocket notebook and another task to list on your calendar.

One Calendar for One Life

Some people tell me they keep two calendars, one for their work life and one for their personal life. This too makes for confusion and a waste of time. You are one person with one life, and you should use one calendar. To the extent that other people's activities affect your life, those activities will also be on your calendar. This is especially true for busy homemakers with several children.

Even though I recommend using just one pocket calendar, it's often very helpful to have a month-by-month calendar as a reference, even one of the five-year varieties, to take a longer view of the months, or years, ahead. Month-by-month calendars are excellent tools for pinpointing vacation times, planning the introduction of a new product, gauging a savings plan for your children's college expenses, outlining the phases of a research study, planning a relocation, or imagining where you want to be in five years. Remember, in Day Two, when I described bite-size brainstorming as, in reality, looking at the big picture? You never want to get so caught up in the minutiae of quarter-hour intervals on your calendar that you can't look at the months and years ahead.

In thinking about your long-term goals, the process is the same: brainstorm the bites of the elephant, organize the bites, and then bring them onto your calendar, whether it be for one year or five years. I always do this in pencil, do lots of erasing and moving around of deadlines until it feels comfortable. To the extent that you intend to perform some of the individual bites for your long-term goal in the current year, you should transfer them onto your pocket calendar.

Calendars are necessary tools for keeping track of your appointments, both external and internal, but they can also help to protect reward time, downtime, private time, Sabbath time, whatever you want to call it. They can help you plan *not to plan*.

Today many people are afflicted with the disease of being too busy, of feeling they must live their lives in the next 20 minutes. I can well identify with their need to be doing fun, stimulating, entertaining, challenging, interesting things every minute of every day. Most of us have jobs, go to school, raise children, have relationships, maintain homes, do volunteer work, and exercise. And many people also enroll in my time management workshops because they don't have enough time!

Friends often complain to me that they feel helpless, controlled by external forces—that their whole lives already seem planned *for* them. Even though it's the first of October, they know exactly what they'll be doing on the fifth of August. "It's so depressing," a woman confessed to me. "It's only March, but already I know too much about what I'll be doing and where I'll be in a year from now." In May she was having trouble finding a store that already had calendars for the next year in stock.

I'm sure it's obvious that these overly busy individuals have made their own beds. However, as an alternative to throwing away their calendars, moving "back to the land," and living by the sun and the seasons, these calendar compulsives can change their schedules if they really want to.

First, it's important to point out here that your pocket calendar is not your "to do" list. You should *not* write a task next to every time interval. You will find overcrowded calendar spaces very defeating. Let the white spaces shine through. It will give you a feeling of flexibility and thus greater control. Second, you can also take a more active approach to keeping your calendar uncluttered.

Carve Out Unplanned Time

In keeping with a principal tenet of the five-day system, start out *small*. Begin by flipping through your pocket calendar pages and locating a free evening—some blank space that you haven't yet filled. Draw a line through it, and let that line be a visual signal to you: do not commit yourself to anything except how you really want to spend that time—with your family, with close friends, or by yourself. I know couples who have regular dates during the week and who get out of town several weekends a year. You can argue that it's too bad people have to schedule time together, but the fact is that the days of a *Father Knows Best* family, where Dad comes home every night at 6:00 P.M. to a stay-at-home spouse, a home-cooked meal, and the scrubbed faces of his children, are gone. My point is simply that it's possible to use your calendar to inject some sanity into your overcrowded schedule.

Similarly, draw a line through a whole day and then an entire weekend. Stand firm and protect these times; don't let other people's demands encroach upon them. If your calendar is already very full, you may have to go way into the future to find uncommitted time, but that's okay. Many of my workshop participants report that unplanning brings balance to their busy, stressful lives.

"It was like a wonderful gift," said a school superintendent and the father of four. "My free weekend arrived and I chose to spend it quietly with time for fishing by myself and time one-on-one with two of my kids and then with my wife. I felt in control and pleased with myself because I hadn't given in to requests to do things with other people."

Students in my workshops who have started to carve out chunks of unplanned time confess to a certain anxiety. One woman called it "fear of the void."

"I'm so used to having 20 million things to do, to going in 10 different directions, to being productive all the time, that at first it was very unsettling to be staring at several unplanned hours," she recalled. "I wrung my hands, I paced the floor, I looked out the window a lot, then I lay down to take a nap."

Is relaxing hard work? No, but it can produce anxiety at first if you're not used to it. Fortunately, the woman didn't give in to her compulsive instincts and tackle some of the tasks in her pocket notebook. The next time she had some unplanned time she read a book, took a walk outside, caught up with a neighbor she hadn't talked to in ages, and just generally let things happen.

Fortunately, rewarding yourself, relaxing, "unplanning," doing nothing, being spontaneous—whatever you want to call it—is highly contagious. The woman who wrung her hands the first time she unplanned never went through that turmoil again. Now she routinely unplans. "My life is much more balanced now," she said. "I still feel pressure from deadlines, but I know that some unplanned time is never far away. I can see where I've blocked it out on my calendar, and I don't let anything intrude."

Guard Against Interruptions

The question I'm asked more frequently than any other is "How do I guard against interruptions?" You can protect yourself against invasion with well-known military tactics: (1) by installing a deep moat around the castle—a protective secretary or a locked door that reads "Do not disturb"; (2) by cutting enemy communications—screening telephone calls, using an answering machine, or taking the phone off the hook; and (3) by using a surefire defense weapon, one that has been called the single most effective time management tool—the word *no*. When all else fails, retreat to a new fortress—your branch library, a town park, an empty conference room at the office—where you are totally removed from all distractions.

A newly elected mayor asked me how to manage the endless barrage of phone calls from the townspeople. He wanted to be responsive to his constituents, but he also wanted to keep his campaign promises, and to solve the town's problems required blocks of uninterrupted time.

I suggested the mayor's secretary say, "Mr. Jones returns phone calls after 4:00 p.m. Can he reach you then?" Of course, in an emergency, the police chief or fire chief could be put right through.

For those who don't have a protective secretary, I recommend using an answering machine, even when you're able to answer the phone. Or, for people who practice behavior that says, "I must take this call because I have to know who it is," I suggest the next time the phone rings and you're in the middle of an important task that you say to yourself repeatedly, "If it's important, whoever it is will call back."

A graphic artist, Jean M., went to work at a small advertising agency where all the employees kept their office doors open. "Unfortunately, an open door sends a signal, 'Come right in.' I was too afraid to offend my colleagues and simply close the door," she recalled. "So I scribbled a note—something like 'crazed artist in pursuit of deadline; do not disturb except in case of fire'—and tacked it on my door, which I then closed. No one disturbed me at all. Later, when I emerged for a coffee break, two colleagues inquired in a teasing jest how the crazed artist was coming along. It was clear they respected my wishes and were not at all put off. In fact, the idea has caught on, and we have sort of an office competition for clever quips on people's closed doors."

Learn the Right Way to Say No

As I said earlier, the word no is a very effective time management tool, but saying it is often more easily preached than practiced. Without going into a lengthy discussion on individual assertiveness, most people say yes to a request for their time because they want people to like them. Often this translates into putting other people's needs ahead of their own.

Just like learning any new behavior, saying no gets easier with practice. But for the squeamish there's a halfway approach that my workshop participants have found very effective. The next time someone calls to ask you to serve on the committee, chair the task force, bake for the bake sale, price for the tag sale, set up for the concert, sell tickets to the play, collect donations for the fund drive, take the inventory, or decorate the gym, you might say "I'm not sure if I have the time. I will think about it and call you back in 24 hours."

Notice that you haven't said no. You've simply said you need time to examine the other demands on your time, time to think it over. Most often people know immediately whether they want to say yes or no. But the postponed reply gives you time to gather your courage, rehearse your regrets, and quite possibly think of someone else to suggest to the caller.

Do you fear the extra time might weaken your resolve? My research shows the opposite is true: when people take 24 hours to think it over, they become firm in their conviction to say no.

If you can refer the caller to another source for the help or work sought, he or she will be forever in your debt, and you will have the satisfaction of not leaving the caller empty-handed.

"I always try to refer the caller to another source," says Barbara A., a busy free-lance writer. "I find my writing colleagues appreciate it, but so does the calling editor, who doesn't have to go back to square one. Instead I've given him a likely prospect. Even though I'm giving business away, I find those referrals pay dividends many times over."

Here are two sample dialogues where the respondent says no, each one a little differently.

CALLER: Hi, Larry.

RECEIVER: Hi, Paul.

CALLER: Larry, I'm calling to ask your help with the Neighborhood Association's recycling program. Can you give me a Saturday morning each month to help sort paper, metal, and glass before it's carted away? It's a great activity for the whole family.

RECEIVER: Gee, Paul, I'm with you in spirit, but I don't have time to help you Saturday mornings right now.

CALLER: Oh, it doesn't take long, only an hour or two at the most, and if you bring some family members, it goes even faster.

RECEIVER: Thanks for asking, Paul, but I'm not a good candidate this time. Good luck, though.

CALLER: Thanks, Larry. Bye.

CALLER: Hi, Virginia.

RECEIVER: Hello, Louise.

CALLER: Virginia, I'm calling to invite you to participate on a business panel for the Chamber of Commerce in December. The panel will focus on banking issues for small-business owners, and we want you, as a lending officer, to address opportunities and procedures for getting loans. The date is December 2.

RECEIVER: Louise, what's the time frame?

CALLER: There's coffee at 10:30, and the panel will start around 11:00, with lunch following at noon.

RECEIVER: Virginia, I'm very busy due to the bank reorganization, so I'd like to take a day to think it over. Thank you for thinking of me—I'm very flattered—and I promise to call you tomorrow.

CALLER: That's fine. I certainly hope you'll say yes. You're our first choice.

RECEIVER: I promise to let you know tomorrow. Good-bye.

The next day:

VIRGINIA: Hello, Louise? It's Virginia.

LOUISE: Hi, Virginia.

VIRGINIA: I'm sorry I won't be able to help you out on your panel in December, but we have two other loan officers here who are not reporting to the president on this reorganization, and I bet one of them would have some time to help you.

LOUISE: Do you think so? Gee, that would be great. How do I call them?

VIRGINIA: Try Doug Smith or Susan Reed at this number. Tell them I suggested you call.

LOUISE: Thanks, Virginia. We'll miss having you, but thanks for these leads.

VIRGINIA: You're welcome. I hope they can help. Bye.

It's important to point out that getting organized may very well leave you with time to donate to an organization you've always wanted to support but never had the time. Getting organized will give you the opportunity to say yes!

Ask Your Friends to Make You Accountable

People who seek advice from time management experts often lead frenetic lives, filled with too many demands. In addition, persons with too much time on their hands, with not enough to do in a day, also need help getting organized so they can identify some goals and put more meaning in their lives. Both kinds of individuals can use the five-day system and both can choose to implement the bites of their elephants by making internal appointments with themselves on their calendars.

However, it will probably come as no surprise that the appointments people most often sabotage are the ones they make with themselves. They allow outside interruptions to invade their creative-thinking time or their reward time much more frequently than their external appointments. Why is that so? It's not just that someone lacks personal assertiveness. An external appointment has an ingredient that is usually lacking in an internal appointment: accountability to another person. Barring an emergency, you don't let a phone call interrupt a meeting with six other people. Likewise, you don't invite a drop-in visitor to sit down and chew the fat while you're on a long-distance call with your boss. At home you ban the kids from the kitchen while you talk to the builder who's about to knock down walls and remodel.

What can you do to better ensure that you'll keep your internal appointments? Ask your friends to help. You can make yourself accountable for the goals you set by getting together with a friend, or a group of friends, to share goals and progress reports. It's easy to procrastinate by yourself; it's much more difficult when you make a commitment to others.

When I first got into the writing business, a friend and I did some research for a medical publisher. Carol and I did our work independently, but we met every Friday to compare notes. Whereas I might have been tempted to procrastinate on my share of the project until the last minute, there was no way I was going to disappoint Carol at our weekly meetings. Call it peer pressure, one-upmanship, or accountability, we completed our work in even segments on time because we had to face each other once a week. And I have never forgotten the benefits of that strategy.

Donald R., the bank president introduced in Day One, wants to begin an exercise program in earnest. An exercise dropout from the school of good intentions, he's decided to let the idea of accountability help him get in shape. Every other evening Donald meets two other men from his neighborhood, and the three walk together. Don used to beat himself up mentally for not running 10 miles a day or completing a rigorous Nautilus course every day at noon. Now he's found a compromise that he can live with, and he's got two buddies who have set the same goal.

A homemaker I know transplants her garden perennials with a friend, and then they go to the friend's yard. Accomplishing half the work in half the time, as well as gaining camaraderie, makes for a foolproof solution to her procrastination tendencies. An elementary school teacher has a grading party with several colleagues in her apartment complex. And this book was written thanks to the regular monthly support of two fellow writers who made me accountable for the chapters I promised to produce.

Take a moment to look again at your lists of tasks from Day Three. Can you identify the ones that do not have specific deadlines imposed from the outside? Can you think of another person, a partner, or several friends who could help you accomplish those jobs, either by actually helping you or by meeting with you regularly to lend support, give encouragement, and spur you on? In the exercise below, name some tasks—perhaps ones that you repeatedly put off—that you could accomplish using this strategy, along with the person(s) you have in mind.

Procrastination Prevention

Task   *Persons to Make Me Accountable*

_____   _____

_____   _____

_____   _____

_____   _____

_____   _____

Work Backward from Your Deadline

Writing deadlines on your calendar, and the steps on the way to getting there, prevents what I call "term paper syndrome." Remember when you had a lengthy paper to write and you put it off until the last minute and pulled an "all-nighter" to get it done on time? Writing the milestones to completing a project in your pocket calendar, spaced out with reasonable time for completion in between, is a sure antidote to all that stress, anxiety, and lack of sleep.

The way to plot the steps in a project, or bites of an elephant, on your calendar is to start at the finish line—that is, write in the deadline—and walk backward.

An example is the production schedule for a newsletter. If you make the finish line (that is, the deadline) the date the newsletter is mailed, then your backward steps look like this:

Mail newsletter

Affix labels

Print newsletter

Final approval of mechanicals

Layout

Proof typesetting

Typeset copy

Proof copy

Copy deadline

If this were your project, you would enter these steps at appropriate intervals on your calendar. Be sure to allow some cushion time, extra padding for flexibility, in case the unexpected happens: your original copy is delayed in coming in, the printer is late, the labels have to be redone, or any other contingency arises.

The strategy of walking backward can be very helpful to people who habitually don't allow enough time for a task. High school students who can't leave the house in time to meet the bus need to list everything they have to do from waking up to leaving the house. Doing this exercise is always an eye-opener.

One woman who attended a workshop exclaimed, "It's no wonder I was late for work every morning. I assumed I could put the mail out for the mailman, put the dog in his pen, set the security system, find my car keys, turn the answering machine on, run a comb through my hair one last time, find my umbrella, check my briefcase, and lower the thermostat, all in five minutes. It takes me much longer than that to leave the house for the day. Now I plan for these tasks by starting the countdown earlier."

Dual-career couples I've met express frustration that they seldom accomplish everything they want to do on the weekend. When they outline their weekend agendas, I'm aghast at their expectations. They're totally unrealistic. They don't allow for the everyday facts of life that slow them down, like dealing with Saturday traffic, waiting in long lines, running to the bank for more cash, starting a car that's slow to get going, and so on. When they go through the exercise of starting at the finish line (the time they want to return home from all their errands) and walking backward, even if they manage only to figure in a reasonable driving time between points, they can reduce their expectations.

Children can learn this kind of step-by-step planning when they first begin to have homework assignments. When my son has to write a book report, for example, we talk about walking backward from the due date so that he does a little each day, in addition to his work for his other subjects. His plan for an oral book report, accompanied by artwork, might look like this:

Friday:	Book report due
Thursday:	
Wednesday:	Write outline for oral report
Tuesday:	Draw poster
Monday:	Finish reading book

Notice that Thursday evening is saved as a cushion, which will most likely be used for practicing his oral report but is available for extra time on the poster if that proves necessary.

A fourth-grader's book report is a very elementary example. There are three "finish lines" below. What are the milestones to reaching them? (This *is* like eating an elephant one bite at a time, but taken the next step: you're assigning an order to the bites and saying how much time each bite will take.)

1. You're giving a surprise party for your best friend on June 1.

_____

_____

_____

_____

_____

_____

2. You're leaving the country for a six-month assignment on September 1 and renting your apartment while you're gone.

_____

_____

_____

_____

_____

_____

3. **You're in charge of publicity for a new play being premiered in a newly renovated theater on January 15.**

_____

_____

_____

_____

_____

_____

_____

_____

_____

_____

_____

Know When to Stop

As I have discussed earlier, it's the big jobs that overwhelm most people. It's the drudgery—cleaning the basement, reorganizing the attic, clearing the garage, reviewing the files—that they put off. And when they brainstorm them and put the tasks in their notebooks, they're still left with the big "do": clean the basement. You can use the suggestions in this book—make an appointment with yourself, get a friend to help, give yourself a big reward—but the best strategy for getting it done is to "eat the elephant one bite at a time," that is, do a little bit at a time.

Charlie M., who sells cars for a living but restores old ones as a hobby, told me that one weekend he resolved to go into his three-car garage on Saturday morning and not come out again until Sunday, when the garage was cleaned out, which is exactly what he did. When he emerged late Sunday afternoon, Charlie had an immaculate garage, but he was also very tired and cross that he hadn't done anything else all weekend. His family was annoyed with him, and what's more, Charlie faced returning to work Monday morning without the benefit of any rest or recreation over the weekend.

Charlie would have been smarter if he had devoted a couple of hours on Saturday and Sunday to his garage and spent the rest of the weekend doing what weekends were originally intended for. He would have needed several weekends to finish the work, but he would be enjoying a more balanced life.

Tackling any elephant a bite at a time is usually a much more satisfying way to accomplish a goal like Charlie's. And it brings up an important point about *stopping* on time. Some people have trouble being somewhere or starting something on time, usually because they don't value it highly or because they don't allow enough time to arrive at that finish line (I leave "rebelling against authority" to the psychologists), but other people aren't tuned in to stopping on time. These are the men and women who take my workshops and complain about staying at work too late.

If Charlie sets a reasonable goal of starting on his garage for three hours Saturday morning, and after three hours he's really on a roll and thinking, "Hey, this isn't so bad. Look at what I've done. I want to keep going," should he stop? There's no hard-and-fast answer, but my experience, and that of hundreds of my workshop participants, suggests that Charlie will be happier over time if he stops working on the garage after three hours. He can congratulate himself on his morning's work, enjoy the reward he planned for himself—which helps to sustain his interest, morale, and motivation until his next garage appointment—and then move on.

How do you stop what you're doing? Many people I know who work at home set a timer or an alarm. Participants in my workshops who wanted to start leaving their offices on time have had a friend or spouse call them to make them accountable. Charlie asked his wife to come to the garage and remind him it was time to leave.

All of these strategies—unplanning, walking backward, eating an elephant one bite at a time—can help you have a calmer, more balanced life. In Charlie's words, "They took me from the pressure cooker into the hot tub."

Problem Calendars

Below are three pages from three separate pocket calendars. What's wrong with them?

7:00 A.M.	
8:00	Eye doctor
9:00	
10:00	
11:00	
12:00 noon	Lunch with Steve
1:00 P.M.	
2:00	Executive Committee
3:00	
4:00	
5:00	
6:00	Squash game
7:00	
8:00	
9:00	

Problems: _____

7:00 A.M.	Breakfast with Stew
8:00	Editorial board
9:00	Production meeting
10:00	Budget meeting
11:00	"
12:00 noon	College alumni lunch
1:00 P.M.	
2:00	Staff meeting
3:00	Review direct mail campaign with Joan

4:00	Meeting with Ted, Glenn, and Peter
5:00	Dictate recommendations re editorial, production, budget, direct mail
6:00	"
7:00	"
8:00	"
9:00	"

Problems: _____

7:00 A.M.	
8:00	
9:00	Tommy takes $2.25 to school Buy new boots for Tommy and Jim
10:00	Take dog to vet
11:00	Pick up sitter Dry cleaner, pharmacy, hardware store
12:00 noon	Lunch with Joan—hurray!
1:00 P.M.	
2:00	Tommy is dropped home by Suzanne, take sitter home
3:00	Drive Gymboree car pool, pick up John's slacks from tailor, rent videotape
4:00	Piano tuner comes
5:00	
6:00	
7:00	
8:00	Kids in bed, watch video
9:00	

Problems: _____

The first calendar consists of only external appointments. The owner is not getting the full benefit of this important organizing tool.

In the next example, one can assume "College alumni lunch" is a reward, which is a positive sign. This calendar user has also made an internal appointment, "dictate recommendations." On the down side, there are too many meetings scheduled back-to-back, not enough planned rewards, and four hours is much too long to spend on dictating. You can be certain this manager's dictating quantity and quality will diminish noticeably without scheduled breaks.

The author of the third calendar had included two planned rewards, "lunch with Joan" and "watch video" and has not packed her day too tightly. The only omission is an internal appointment.

In structuring your uncommitted time vis-à-vis your bites, don't pack your days too tightly. You must have room for the unexpected. On the other hand, don't be so loose that there's not enough substance to provide a sense of momentum, a sense that you're in control and that you're moving forward. Through trial and error you will find the right balance for *you*.

The following pages are for *your* calendar. Begin by entering the external appointments that you have. Next, look for the wide-open spaces, the uncommitted blocks of time. From your lists of calls, errands, things to do, and things to write, make internal appointments with yourself to accomplish some of these tasks. Remember to include specific rewards and unplanned time. Record any deadlines, either external or internal, that you have and walk backward from them, writing down the steps you need to take to get there.

And finally, remember that as much as writing things down brings you closer to making it happen, everything should be viewed as flexible or subject to change. You can change your mind at any time.

Your Calendar

6:00 A.M.——————————————————

7:00——————————————————————

8:00——————————————————————

9:00——————————————————————

10:00—————————————————————

11:00—————————————————————

12:00 noon————————————————

1:00 P.M.———————————————————

2:00——————————————————————

3:00——————————————————————

4:00——————————————————————

5:00——————————————————————

6:00——————————————————————

7:00——————————————————————

8:00——————————————————————

9:00——————————————————————

10:00—————————————————————

11:00—————————————————————

Your Calendar

6:00 A.M._____

7:00_____

8:00_____

9:00_____

10:00_____

11:00_____

12:00 noon_____

1:00 P.M._____

2:00_____

3:00_____

4:00_____

5:00_____

6:00_____

7:00_____

8:00_____

9:00_____

10:00_____

11:00_____

Congratulations! You've just completed Day Four to getting organized. Remember to reward your good work.

DAY 4

☑ ☑ ☑ ☑ ☐

1. Record external appointments (deadlines imposed by the outside world).

2. Identify blocks of time on your calendar, identify appropriate tasks from your pocket notebook, and make appointments with yourself for those blocks of time.

3. Write down planned rewards.

4. Block out unplanned time.

5. Write your deadlines on your calendar.

Give yourself a reward!

The Daily
"To Do" List

Four days down and one to go—you're almost there. At this point you should feel a lot more organized already, because you have identified rewards, bite-size brainstormed your elephants, grouped the tasks into categories, and written some of them on your calendar. These steps will become automatic with practice.

Every time you think of a reward you would like, you write it on the rewards page in your notebook. When you encounter an elephant, you break it down into bites and put those bites in your notebook as well. When you have a meeting, an appointment, or a social engagement, you write that on your calendar. You also pinpoint uncommitted blocks of time and make internal appointments with yourself to do tasks from your notebook. You also insert planned rewards into your calendar pages. All that remains is to write, once a day, a daily "to do" list.

Why not just refer to your notebook in planning your day? After all, your notebook is your entire "to do" list. The reason is simple. Your pocket notebook contains too many tasks to do in one day, and reading through the notebook every time you're ready to do something new takes too much time. Besides, trying to use a list that long on a daily basis is likely to put you off; that approach is simply not conducive to *doing* anything.

Why not use your calendar as a daily "to do" list? As I said in Day Four, I don't recommend writing a task next to every quarter hour. As so many of my workshop participants have pointed out, to look at an overcrowded calendar several times a day, just like a very full pocket notebook, is very defeating and can give you a feeling of being overwhelmed and out of control. For people who complain that Monday's "to do" list becomes Tuesday's, which becomes Wednesday's, and so on, the never-ending cycle of rewriting the same tasks on each calendar page and having to look at that over and over can be very depressing.

In reality, your notebook and your calendar are your mental file cabinets: you write in them the things you want to remember, whenever they come up. Once a day, either first thing in the morning or last thing in the evening, you open both of these file cabinets and, choosing from them, write your daily "to do" list. Your daily list can be written on a piece of scratch paper or use a back page of your notebook; it is then thrown away at the end of the day.

Start with Internal and External Appointments

Begin by copying down the external and internal appointments from the calendar page for that day. For example, on Day Four you saw a calendar page for Jim R.:

Tuesday

Susan and Luke's anniversary

7:30 A.M.	Breakfast meeting with Ted
9:30 A.M.	Staff meeting
10:45 A.M.	Draft new marketing strategy
12:30 P.M.	Lunch in the park
1:30 P.M.	Meet with purchasing
2:30 P.M.	Review personnel policies handbook
6:30 P.M.	Dinner with my wife
8:00 P.M.	"Go to School" night

Add Some Tasks from Your Pocket Notebook

Jim is already anticipating quite a full day, but in the last 15 minutes before he leaves his office on Monday he leafs through the pages of his pocket notebook and chooses a few tasks—some calls, errands, things to do, and things to write—that he also wants to accomplish on Tuesday. His "to do" list for Tuesday looks like this:

Tuesday

Susan and Luke's anniversary

7:30 A.M.   Breakfast meeting with Ted

Stop by post office for new issue (the post office is on the route between the restaurant where the breakfast meeting will take place and Jim's office, and Jim collects stamps as a hobby)

Call Luke to confirm weekend plans

Call Milt at car dealership

Pick up health insurance info from Sam (to take to the staff meeting)

9:30 A.M.   Staff meeting

Pick up copies of last marketing plan from Carol

10:45 A.M.   Draft new marketing strategy

12:30 P.M.   Lunch in the park

Buy extra tent stakes from camping store (between Jim's office and the park and next to the deli where he buys lunch to go)

1:30 P.M.   Meet with purchasing

2:30 P.M.   Review personnel policies handbook

Write memo to department heads: personnel policies recommendations due in one week before meeting

Do travel expense voucher

6:30 P.M.   Dinner with my wife

8:00 P.M.   "Go to School" night

You might ask, "When does Jim return phone calls? When does he go through his mail, at the office and at home?" Jim doesn't put on his "to do" list the things he does automatically, like looking at his mail or returning phone calls. Again, he writes down what he wants to remember.

Jim's meeting with his purchasing department at 1:30 won't necessarily last until his internal appointment at 2:30, and he can use any time in between to answer calls or read the mail. If the purchasing meeting does take the whole hour, or more, he has some flexibility between 2:30 and 6:30 and can reevaluate the tasks he planned to do in the afternoon.

ORGANIZATIONAL MYTH No. 9: *"I should never put off until tomorrow what I can do today."*

When Jim reads the pages of his pocket notebook, how does he decide which tasks to include on his daily "to do" list? Deciding what to do, or setting priorities, is one of the most important factors in getting organized. Whether you realize it or not, in choosing to do one thing and not another, or in choosing to do one thing before another, you set and reevaluate priorities all the time. Some choices result in a feeling of self-satisfaction while others do not. I propose you decide what to do based on how you will *feel* after you do it. In other words, the fact that you *can* do a particular task today doesn't mean you *should*.

Remember the fantasy world with unlimited time? If you didn't have any deadlines, you wouldn't have to make as many choices. You would react to paper and reading matter as you received it. You would react to the phone when it rang and to people when they came by. Yes, sometimes there would be interruptions—I can't even imagine a world without them—such as a visitor stopping in while you are on the phone. But basically everything in this fantasy world would be so laid back that everyone would have time to wait. After all, what would be the rush?

The real world, though, is full of deadlines, and deadlines are, for the most part, good. Because of them you do your work, move forward, and accomplish goals. Also because of deadlines, you are forced to make choices about what to do.

Syndicated columnist Ellen Goodman has written of a contemporary disease she calls "consumeritis." As American consumers, we have too many choices, she says. Take, for example, buying soap. In olden days, one went to the general store and bought a bar of soap. Today you must choose between plain soap and fancy soap; bar soap and soft soap; white soap, pink soap, yellow soap, and green soap; nonallergenic soap, deodorant soap, and so on. Is it any wonder that you stand overwhelmed and consumer-weary in the aisle of your grocery store?

Similarly, people face myriad choices about how to spend their time. As organizing experts have long observed, most people assign a task a high priority—"I must do this today"—because of urgency. You pay the mortgage because it is due on the first of the month, you fill the gas tank because the gauge reads near empty, you write a meeting agenda because the meeting is set for today, you refill your medical prescription because the bottle is empty, and so on. The completion of these tasks gives you a good feeling but doesn't exactly send you into the realm of ecstasy.

It's very important that you also choose to do tasks because you'll feel terrific afterward. These things to do are therefore important but not necessarily urgent. Look back at Jim R.'s "to do" list. Perhaps the most important tasks he has chosen are the stop at the post office, because his stamp collection is a high priority for him, and the trip to the camping store, because camping is a favorite recreation and he and Luke have planned a father-son camping trip for the coming weekend.

Anyone can argue that Jim will feel good when he runs a successful staff meeting, when he drafts a new marketing strategy, and when he has an enjoyable dinner with his wife before "Go to School" night, but *for Jim* the errands to the post office and the camping store are the tasks that will give him the greatest self-satisfaction.

Notice that these tasks will not take up a lot of time compared to the many other projects scheduled into Jim's day. Alan Lakein, a pioneer in the field of life planning, was the first to apply the 80/20 rule to quality of life, in *How to Get Control of Your Time and Your Life.* Mr. Lakein points out that just as salespeople will tell you that 80 percent of their sales revenue comes from 20 percent of their customers, 80 percent of your self-satisfaction results from 20 percent of your activities. In other words, you value that 20 percent of your activities—accomplishing them is worth more to you—more than the other 80 percent.

The most important thing, of course, is to know what you, and only you, value. Consider these examples:

□ *Reviewing the personnel policies handbook is part of Jim R.'s job, but it has low value for him. Maureen E., on the other hand, has been appointed director of personnel for an expanding company that previously had no personnel director. The first elephant she encounters in her newly created position is to review, expand, and publish the company's personnel policies. So the completion of this goal holds a high value for Maureen.*

☐ *Lisa B., a food stylist, has to design and prepare foods for an Easter dinner that will be photographed for a major food magazine in two days. However, this project will yield little value for Lisa, who has decided to change directions and teach cooking to mentally disadvantaged adults and children. In contrast, Sarah S., the mother of three small children, has decided to decorate her dining room for Easter, in addition to preparing dinner for her grown siblings and their small children, and for Sarah the Easter preparations will yield a lot of self-satisfaction.*

☐ *Martha E. looks with disdain at her perennial flower beds, which are starting to be choked by weeds. An investment analyst who purports to love to dig in the earth on weekends, Martha realizes that weed pulling won't provide much self-satisfaction today. A more highly valued activity would be assembling the hammock she has bought her husband for their anniversary and then testing it herself, stretched out with her favorite magazine. Pulling weeds is, however, a highly valued activity for Isabel C., a prizewinning rose grower and horticultural judge.*

☐ *Taking a walk a little farther than he did yesterday will give Rod J., age 75, a lot of self-satisfaction as he recovers from knee surgery, but Sandy H. walks in the park because she knows it's good for her. It's not as personally satisfying for her as writing a paper for her history course, part of getting her college degree after raising her children.*

☐ *Attending a local job fair on his lunch hour holds high value for Mark M., who is dissatisfied with his dead-end job and who faces an imminent rent increase. It is, however, a low priority for Jim Y., who is comfortable with his life as a struggling artist. Painting is Jim's most highly valued activity these days, but he says he'll drop in at the job fair to please his parents.*

Only you know what you value. The point of knowing your values, or priorities, is to make sure every "to do" list includes some high-priority tasks. Completing them gives you a "high" in terms of self-esteem and self-satisfaction. To put it another way, doing what you really want to do makes you feel good. That's how you'll get to the end of a busy day, or a quiet day, and feel satisfied. And day after day after day of feeling satisfied leads to a complete and happy life!

Now take a look at your lists of calls, errands, things to do, and things to write. Consider each item carefully and try to imagine how you will feel about yourself after you've completed the task. You can better clarify what is important in your life by identifying tasks as "have-tos" "want-tos," and "dream-ofs."

Identify Have-to Tasks

Most people can easily identify their have-tos: buy the groceries, pick up the dry cleaning, pay the bills, mow the grass, walk the dog, wash the clothes—the life maintenance chores mentioned earlier. They're usually urgent, they're the stuff of life, but completing them doesn't give you lots of satisfaction. (Of course, you now know that enjoying rewards after completing them is a surefire way to get through them.)

On many days 80 percent of your activities will be have-tos. Remember, these are the tasks that yield only 20 percent of your self-satisfaction. In the space below, list a few tasks you would call have-tos:

Have-tos:

1. _____

2. _____

3. _____

4. _____

5. _____

6. _____

Identify Want-to Tasks

Want-tos are higher on the value scale. Want-tos are just that: things you want to do but don't necessarily have to do. For Jim R., drafting a new marketing strategy is a want-to. No specific deadline has been attached to this task by an outside person or source, but for the company to grow and prosper, the marketing strategy must be drafted, and Jim has given it an internal deadline of six months from now.

The examples on pages 119–120 point to additional want-tos:

☐ Maureen E.   Review, expand, and publish personnel policies.

☐ Sarah S.   Prepare Easter decorations and dinner.

☐ Lisa B.   Get a job working with mentally disadvantaged adults and/or children.

☐ Martha E.   Assemble a hammock, lie in it, and read.

☐ Isabel C.   Weed her garden.

☐ Rod J.   Take a walk.

☐ Sandy H.   Write a history paper.

☐ Mark M.   Attend a job fair.

☐ Jim Y.   Paint pictures.

To feel a sense of self-satisfaction upon reviewing your day—"I spent time on a few activities that really matter to me"—you must include want-tos on every daily "to do" list. Remember, want-tos may comprise only 20 percent of your activities or time, but accomplishing them nets you 80 percent of your satisfaction.

One of my workshop participants gave me her personal definition of a want-to. "It's something I must do regularly because when I don't my whole self is out of sync," she said. One man said he must write in a journal every day, another said he must paint. One woman said if she doesn't ride her bicycle regularly, she's out of balance. Still another man said he must walk at the beach. Want-tos, spoken of in these terms, are often rewards.

Looking again at your lists of tasks, write down several you would label want-tos

Want-tos

1. _____

2. _____

3. _____

4. _____

5. _____

6. _____

Identify Dream-of Tasks

The final type of activity includes the things you dream about doing. These are elephants just like the things you want to do and what you have to do. You can break them down into bites, and you *can* achieve them. Here are some examples of goals my workshop participants have dreamed about:

- ☐ Becoming an actress
- ☐ Learning to fly
- ☐ Taking two weeks of vacation and doing nothing
- ☐ Taking singing lessons
- ☐ Writing a family history
- ☐ Building a house
- ☐ Joining the Peace Corps
- ☐ Getting reconnected with a loved one
- ☐ Starting my own business
- ☐ Writing a letter to the president
- ☐ Having a love affair
- ☐ Building a boat
- ☐ Making a difference in a human problem such as hunger, shelter, or education
- ☐ Producing a play

There are as many different dreams as there are people to dream them, but a dream goal is like a videotape that plays, rewinds, and then plays again. It keeps tugging at your gut, and it won't quit.

Accomplishing a task for a dream goal yields the highest value— it can make you feel like a million—but planning for your dreams is often frightening. You assume the bites to the elephant are activities you've never tried before and therefore you're uncomfortable with them. However, *every* goal—whether it's a have-to, a want-to, or a dream-of—can be broken down into *doing* bites that are calls, errands, things to do, or things to write. The happiest, most fulfilled people (notice I didn't say "most successful") are the ones who dream dreams and then take steps, the same measured steps outlined in this book, to bring them to reality. And these individuals are very organized. They put their dream tasks in their pocket notebooks, in their pocket calendars, and on their daily "to do" lists.

Years after a woman took one of my workshops, I learned of her dream-come-true by dining in her restaurant. A homemaker and a parent, Joan K. had left her job as a sous-chef to raise her kids, all the while dreaming of owning her own restaurant. While being a mom she felt competent about cooking, but she had no idea how to manage a restaurant, buy or rent space, finance the venture, run an ongoing business, etc. Still she continued to dream.

When her children were a little older Joan K. began calling her former restaurant cronies for their advice and know-how. She also investigated hotel and restaurant management courses available at nearby colleges and, when she could afford the time and money, enrolled in some. Little by little, over many years, Joan K. accomplished the bites of her elephant. Often even the individual tasks seemed scary to her, so she conscientiously gave herself a reward after each one. Today, in her early fifties, Joan K. owns one of the top restaurants in Boston.

What videotapes play relentlessly in your mind? What do you dream about doing? Write your dreams below.

Dream-ofs

1. _____

2. _____

3. _____

4. _____

5. _____

6. _____

7. _____

8. _____

9. _____

10. _____

Look at Just Two Choices at a Time

"I understand all the steps you put forth," says Marion W., president of her own public relations firm, "but my entire day is made up of top-priority, high-value tasks. They're all important, they're all urgent, and I waste time agonizing over what to do first." Marion's cry is very common. Having too much to do and not enough time seems like a national disease. In fact, it's the "in" disease today.

But you *do* know which task is more important than another. As so many of the current prophets of intuition ask, how do you feel in your gut? Looking at your list of phone calls in your pocket notebook, for example, ask yourself how you'll feel after you complete the first call on the list. Now consider the second call. Will you feel more or less satisfied in making it than after making the first? If placing the second call will net you more satisfaction than the first, you should make the second call before the first. Now, how does it compare to the third call on the list, and so on?

Look at the following list of calls. What are the top-priority calls for a man who wants to change his career?

Change Careers

Calls

Jim re accounts receivable

Bill for car service appointment

Sara, Ann, Jonathan for off-site brainstorming meeting

*University re career change courses

Dr. Moriarty re eye checkup

*Steve re lunch to talk about opportunites in the insurance field

*"Résumés, Inc.," re costs, etc.

Payroll office for cash advance

PR office to schedule press photo

Assuming the man wants to move ahead on changing his career, completing some of the calls associated with that goal (those with an asterisk) each day is a top priority because of how terrific he will feel after making them. He will add other calls to his daily "to do" list based on urgency and external deadlines.

In another, very different example what are the top-priority errands for a young mother whose goal is to provide enriching experiences for her small children while running her household?

Provide Enriching Experiences for Children

Errands

Dry cleaners
*Visit library children's room
Food shopping
*Pet store, just to look
*Art supply store for modeling clay
Barber shop
Shoe repair shop
Paint store

This mother's top-priority errands include those with an asterisk, the errands that could yield tools for stimulating activities. No doubt her food shopping, dry cleaning, shoe repair, and other errands are urgent, but they are have-tos, or life maintenance tasks. She has to do them, but accomplishing them provides her with a minimal personal satisfaction.

Imagine that you wrote every task on an index card and arranged the cards in order of priority. You *could* make those decisions, and I've encountered busy people who've used this method as a last resort. But carried to this extreme on a regular basis, the priority-setting, or decision-making, process can become compulsive and therefore a time-waster rather than a time-saver. Just as it's possible to become neurotic about making lists and thus never get anything done, it's possible to spend too much time prioritizing. The only cure for decision-making paralysis is to pick a task and do it.

"But I have lots of trouble making decisions," says Ian K., a salesman. "Is there help for people like me?" Just as organizing comes more easily to some people than to others, some people make decisions more easily and quickly than others. However, just as you can learn how to be more organized, you can improve your decision-making skills with practice.

For people like Ian K., I often prescribe what I call "decision warm-up exercises." They're easy and fun, and the trick is to limit your choices at first. For example, very quickly do the exercise below.

I. Check the one you prefer:

Of colors,

☐ (a) red

☐ (b) blue

On vacation,

☐ (a) sun

☐ (b) snow

In music,

☐ (a) classical

☐ (b) rock

Of actors,

☐ (a) Robert Redford

☐ (b) Paul Newman

Of actresses,

☐ (a) Meryl Streep

☐ (b) Glenn Close

Wasn't that easy? Now you increase the number of choices. Remember, do this exercise very fast. No stalling.

II. Check the one you prefer:

Of colors,

    □ (a) red

    □ (b) purple

    □ (c) turquoise

    □ (d) rust

On vacation,

    □ (a) ocean beach

    □ (b) skiing in the Rockies

    □ (c) wilderness camping

    □ (d) Paris in spring

In music,

    □ (a) opera

    □ (b) ragtime

    □ (c) golden oldies

    □ (d) country

Of actors,

    □ (a) Dustin Hoffman

    □ (b) William Hurt

    □ (c) Michael Douglas

    □ (d) Jason Robards, Jr.

Of actresses,

    □ (a) Elizabeth Taylor

    □ (b) Amy Irving

    □ (c) Cicely Tyson

    □ (d) Jane Fonda

The second exercise may be a little more difficult, but it's nevertheless fun and hardly impossible. In the third exercise the number of choices doesn't grow, but the questions become more serious.

III. Check the one you prefer:

Your top priority in a paid job, assuming it's work you enjoy, is

☐ (a) salary

☐ (b) flexible hours

☐ (c) short commute from home

☐ (d) opportunity to move up

When you do volunteer work, what matters most to you is

☐ (a) contributing ideas

☐ (b) hands-on helping

☐ (c) personal publicity

☐ (d) making friends

A personal priority for you right now is

☐ (a) spending more time with your spouse

☐ (b) getting out of a going-nowhere relationship

☐ (c) getting in shape

☐ (d) investigating other career opportunities

Your favorite social setting is

☐ (a) a party of 100 people you've never met

☐ (b) a long, quiet dinner with your best friend

☐ (c) a networking meeting with half friends and half new faces

☐ (d) a reunion of many old friends

The adventure you'd enjoy most is

□ (a) taking a ride in a balloon

□ (b) white-water rafting

□ (c) training wild falcons

□ (d) living in a kibbutz

The point of the exercises is that you must choose *one* priority. I doubt if there's anyone who wouldn't prefer to have a job with flexible hours, a competitive salary, a short commute, and opportunity to move up the ladder, but which one is *most* important to you *now?* In the same way, when you're getting organized and choosing tasks for your daily "to do" list, you must look at your pocket notebook and decide on just a few *important tasks to do that day.*

Work Your Way Up to Looking at Multiple Choices

Friends of mine, Sally M., a homemaker, and Jim M., a product manager, have four children and a house they're outgrowing fast. They want to "trade up" to a larger house, but they can't afford to do so. (Due to town zoning restrictions, they can't add on to their current house.) And yet they do have two cars, take family vacations, and enjoy leisure-time sports and hobbies that cost money. When they complained to me about not being able to decide where to cut back and where to spend, I recommended they list everything they want and then put them in order of priority. Their list looked something like this:

Options

Staying in the same town (versus moving to a lower-priced real estate market)

Having more room

Going camping every summer

Going south every spring

Skiing for long weekends in the winter

Buying new cars every few years

Collecting antiques

Summer programs for the kids

Boating in the summer

Sally's *not* getting a paid job

Jim's *not* changing jobs solely for a higher salary

Sally and Jim didn't need to list everything they spend money on, only the big items. This exercise was not easy, but only by doing it were they (and you) able to make some decisions and then take action. The process doesn't have to be complicated. Just start at the top, compare the first two choices, and place one ahead of the other. Then move to the next option and compare. In the end, Sally and Jim ranked their priorities like this:

1. Sally's *not* getting a paid job.
2. Jim's *not* changing jobs solely for a higher salary.
3. Having more room.
4. Summer programs for the kids.
5. Buying new cars after more than *five* years.
6. Eliminate vacations, boating, and antiques for a few years.

With the help of a competent financial planner, Sally and Jim determine that they can afford the mortgage, upkeep, and expenses of a larger home.

Plot a Graph for Your Biological Clock

In addition to knowing your priorities, understanding your own "biological clock" can help you complete your tasks more effectively. You probably can say whether you are a "morning person," that is, someone whose energy is higher in the morning, or a "night person," someone whose creative juices flow more readily in the afternoon and evening. But there's more to it than that.

If you were to plot the peaks and valleys of your energy throughout 24 hours, what would the graph look like?

Here's the biological clock of Ann B., a homemaker and mother of four:

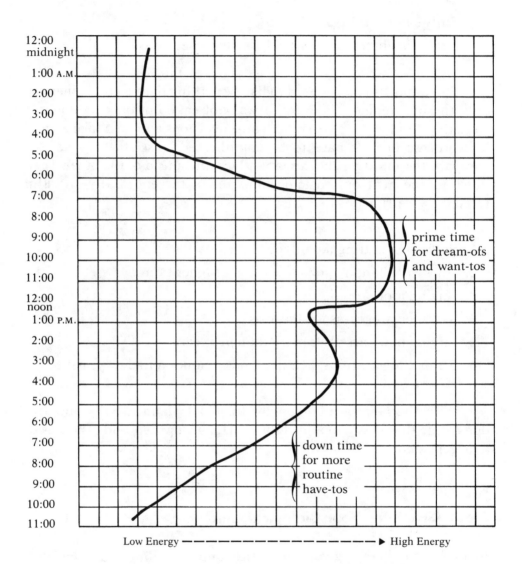

Here's a very different graph for Don E., an engineer:

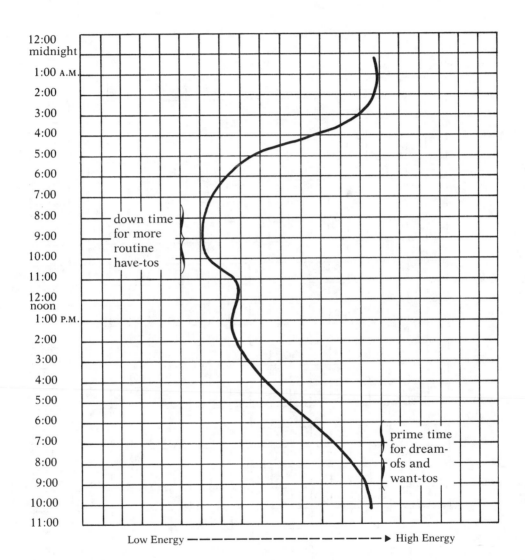

down time
for more
routine
have-tos

prime time
for dream-
ofs and
want-tos

Low Energy — — — — — — — — — — — ► High Energy

Below is a timetable for you to chart. Do you droop after lunch and then rally again in mid-afternoon? Can you do demanding, creative work in the evening? Do you get going in the morning after exercise? However your energy ebbs and flows, show it in the space below.

My Biological Clock Graph

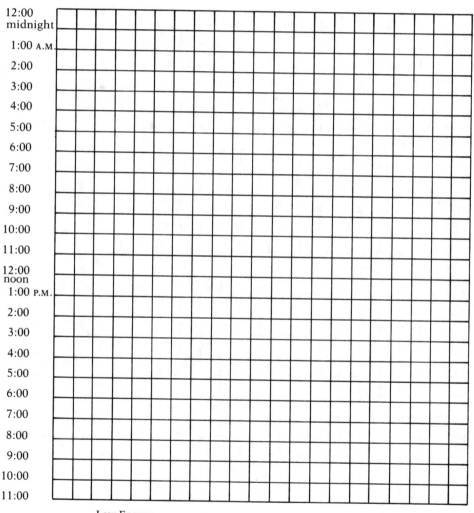

Low Energy ─ ─ ─ ─ ─ ─ ─ ─ ─ ─ ─ ─ ─ ─ ─ ▶ High Energy

This information is helpful in planning the best use of your time. Your periods of peak energy are called "prime time," and you should schedule your want-to and dream-of tasks during this time. When you're more sluggish and less productive, you should do have-to chores. They're usually more routine and don't require much brain-power.

Homemaker Ann B., for example, should schedule her dream-of and want-to tasks in the morning before 12:00 noon, and save her more routine have-tos, which don't require as much energy and brain power, for the afternoon. Just the opposite is true for Don E., who will accomplish more dream-of and want-to tasks if he schedules them during his prime time after 3:00 P.M. and in the evening.

Schedule Your Prioritized Tasks

Does your calendar for next week reflect the best use of your prime time? How could you change your calendar? What would your ideal day be like? When would you do have-tos, want-tos, and dream-ofs? In the timetable below, mark out your ideal have-to, want-to, and dream-of sections.

My Ideal Biological Clock Timetable

12:00 midnight _____

1:00 A.M.   _____

2:00   _____

3:00   _____

4:00   _____

5:00   _____

6:00   _____

7:00   _____

8:00   _____

9:00   _____

10:00	_____
11:00	_____
12:00 noon	_____
1:00 P.M.	_____
2:00	_____
3:00	_____
4:00	_____
5:00	_____
6:00	_____
7:00	_____
8:00	_____
9:00	_____
10:00	_____
11:00	_____

Include High Priorities on Every "To Do" List

As you go through a day and do the work on your "to do" list, you cross off the items you complete. You cross them off in your pocket notebook as well. "But what does it mean when I repeatedly see the same tasks *not* crossed off in my notebook?" asked Carol G., a marketing executive. "I really *want to* buy some new furniture and fix up my apartment, I really *want to* have my new neighbors over for dinner, I really *want to* organize all my snapshots from the last few years—these tasks are in my notebook but they never *leave* my notebook. Why?"

If you're spending too much time on have-tos and other low-priority tasks, and you're feeling dissatisfied as a result, the solution is to make sure every daily "to do" list includes one or two high-priority tasks. If this is hard to do by yourself, ask a friend to help you be accountable.

Delegate

No system of getting organized is complete without a word on delegating. Often at war with perfectionism, delegation is easy to preach but sometimes difficult to practice. Susan B., a team leader at an alternative school for troubled teens, complained, "I have five teachers under my supervision and a mammoth amount of administrative paperwork, but I'm such a perfectionist, I can't even delegate the work that pertains to their classes, which should rightfully be theirs."

Fellow participants in the organizing workshop Susan attended suggested she eat an elephant one bite at a time, that is, do a brainstorm for her paperwork load and then start out small: assign one small task to just one teacher and then work up to more. Susan was also reminded to start at the finish line and walk backward, that is, assign the subordinate teacher a deadline well before Susan's deadline in case revisions proved necessary.

While delegating may be difficult in your daily routine, I am often amazed at how quickly people can delegate in times of personal crisis. When serious illness strikes, devoted mothers can farm out their kids to friends and attend the sick, and conscientious fathers can skip business meetings that were supposedly "can't miss" appointments and send a colleague in their place.

Imagine that you have all your current responsibilities but are suddenly hospitalized. Whom will you ask to do your work? Look back at Jim R.'s daily "to do" list for Tuesday. If you were Jim, whom could you ask to do each of those tasks? Look at your list of errands. Imagine that you *had* to delegate them. Whom would you give them to? Complete the exercise below.

Tasks to Delegate   **Delegated to Whom?**

1. _____

2. _____

3. _____

4. _____

5. _____

6. _____

Tasks to Delegate   **Delegated to Whom?**

7. _____

8. _____

9. _____

10. _____

Delegating is a very effective tool for getting rid of have-tos and perhaps lightening the load of your want-tos. That way you can spend more time on what you dream about doing.

Learn to Let Go

Besides failing to include high-priority activities in your day, it's also possible that what you once thought was important to you no longer is. I call the process of discovering this "creative procrastination."

ORGANIZATIONAL MYTH NO. 10: *"I should never let go of a task once I've listed it as a thing to do."*

This is simply not true. When you have practiced the Five Days method for a while, you will notice the items that you never cross off your lists. It's important to learn from the tasks that keep staring back at you. Are you procrastinating? Maybe not. You could be letting go. The conclusion to be drawn is that these tasks just aren't important enough to you. Either don't do them at all or get someone else to do them.

What can you let go of? What projects or tasks do you know deep down that you'll never get around to? Write them below.

Tasks to Let Go Of

1. _____

2. _____

3. _____

4. _____

5. _____

6. _____

When you recognize the good that can come out of creative procrastination, or letting go of what doesn't matter anymore, you can see that while the organizing process is a fixed framework, the values, goals, tasks, and rewards inside it are all in a state of flux. You can change your mind at any time, as most people do when they grow and change and evolve.

One word of caution, however: your feelings of self-satisfaction will not be served by letting go of too many wants and dreams, although occasionally you might choose it, based on what are realistic expectations. Joan K., the restaurateur, had always dreamed of becoming fluent in French, but she's let go of that and hired waiters who speak it. But more importantly, Joan has delegated to professionals her financial affairs, the care of her home, and even the selection of her clothing. Spending her time operating her restaurant yields the highest personal satisfaction for Joan.

Use a Spider-gram — and Be Brutal

There's another very helpful tool for simplifying your life, a "spider-gram," shown to me by another organizing consultant. A spider-gram is a way to look at the whole big picture of your life and all the people and things that make demands on our time. The oval, or body of the spider, represents *you*. Each leg represents anything in your life that takes your time. For example:

spouse	house	church/temple
friends	yard	volunteer work
kids	pet	entertaining
parents	car	desk work
in-laws	job	shopping
sports	exercise	hobbies

The spider-gram for Fred C., a TV station manager, looks like this:

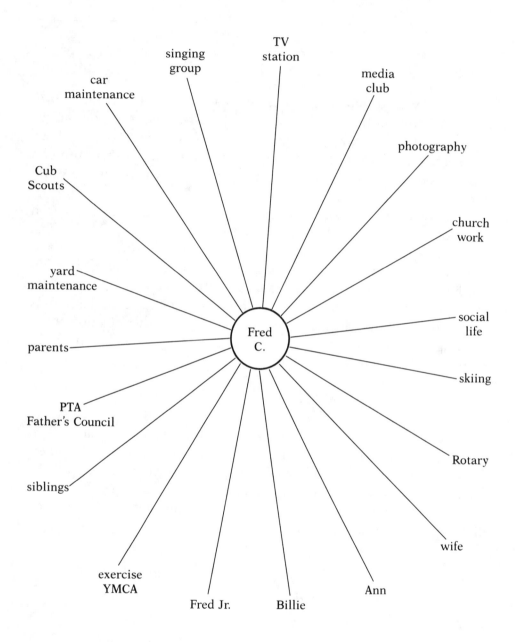

Using one person, thing, or activity for each leg of the spider, draw the "legs" of your life. Be as specific as you can. If you have more than one hobby, each one should be a separate leg.

Spider-gram

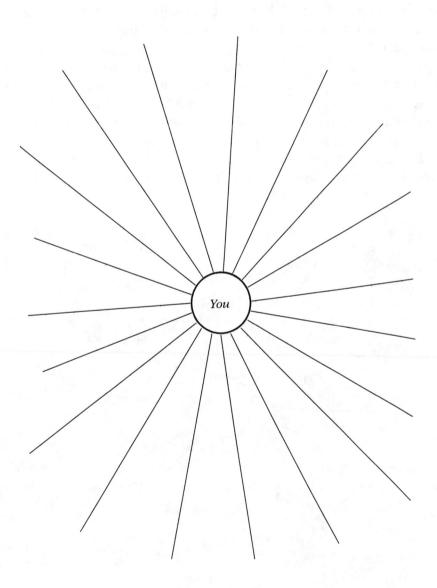

A real spider has only eight legs, but most of my workshop participants discover their spider-grams have dozens of legs. "No wonder I feel overwhelmed and overprogrammed," cried Fred C., a TV station manager. "I'm involved in too many things, so everything, including my family, is getting short shrift." Fred C. enrolled in my workshop because he thought he was disorganized. "I'm not disorganized," he exclaimed. "I just have too much to do!"

The answer for anyone who complains of carrying around too many legs is to cut some off. Sound like a brutal tactic? It is, but it's the only way I know of to simplify your life and focus on what you value most.

Helen R., in contrast to people whose lives are overburdened with legs, has recently relocated to a new state to make a fresh start following a divorce. She wants to make friends and to become involved in her community—in other words, to add legs. Most people would envy Helen her unencumbered life.

By following the steps outlined in this book to enrich her life, Helen R. imagines a spider-gram that looks like this:

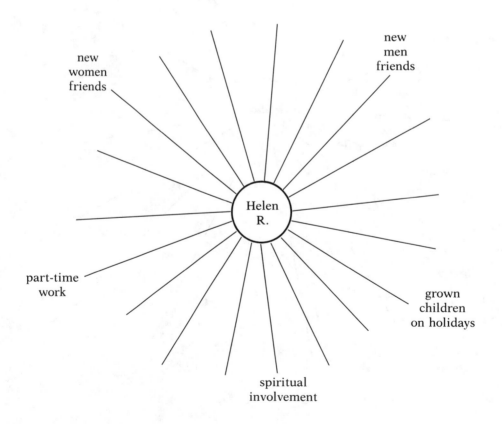

Write a "To Do" List for Tomorrow

Now that you know how to set priorities based on how you will feel after completing a task, you can write your daily "to do" list.

Keeping the instructions in this chapter in mind, write your "to do" list for tomorrow in the space below. Getting organized is like learning to swing a golf club correctly, to ski, or to ride a bicycle: you have to keep a lot of points in mind at the same time. But as with golfing, skiing, and cycling, repeated practice makes you more proficient.

Tomorrow's "To Do" List

_____

_____

_____

_____

_____

_____

_____

_____

_____

_____

_____

_____

_____

_____

_____

_____

_____

_____

_____

_____

_____

Congratulations! You're organized! And if you take a few minutes each day to follow the steps outlined in *Five Days,* you'll stay that way. Now that you have a plan, all that remains is to get started. Remember that being organized is not the end—it's the beginning!

DAY 5

☑ ☑ ☑ ☑ ☑

1. List internal and external appointments from your pocket calendar.

2. Choose tasks to add from your pocket notebook.
   ☐ Be sure to include rewards.

   ☐ Include at least one high-priority (highly satisfying) task.

   ☐ Limit them to a realistic number.

3. Schedule the tasks according to your biological clock — highly valued want-to activities during your "prime time," have-tos when you typically have less energy.

4. Cross out tasks from your "to do" list and your pocket notebook as you complete them.

5. Let go of tasks that appear routinely and are never completed. If necessary, cut some "legs" out of your life.

Give yourself a reward!

Five-Day
Wrap-up

In the Introduction to this book I asked you to write down why you want to get organized. What do you want to change? What are your ruts? What are your time problems? Having read this book and completed the exercises, do you understand how to get what you want out of life, and do you have a plan for achieving that?

Most of the participants in my time management workshops learn the techniques outlined in this book and go on to lead happier, more productive lives. Almost all of them agree that doing their tasks is simple once they have a plan.

"It all looks so much smaller written down," remarked Alec L., an editor. "Now I know exactly where to begin," echoes Jane M., a mechanical artist. Happily, most people who learn and practice sound organizing skills get where they want to go and have a lot of fun along the way.

It's human nature, however, to fall off the track once in a while. When you become caught up in unexpected events, you can lose sight of rewards, goals, and priorities and experience what I call a "write-off day," a write-off week, month, or even year—times when you just survive. Fortunately, it's always possible to try again, to get reorganized and back into gear.

The simple diamond-shaped diagram below can remind you of the steps in the five-day method. (It's a good idea to copy it into your pocket notebook for quick reference!)

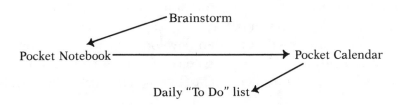

If you've gotten organized and you're still stuck—you can't get started on a task you've chosen, ask yourself these questions, which follow the five-day framework:

1. Have you planned a reward? If not, you must identify a specific reward that will immediately follow the completion of the task.

2. Is the job too big? If it is, then make sure you break the elephant down into the smallest possible "bites."

3. Are you trying to remember too much? Write it all down.

4. Is the task in a jumble with too many other tasks? Organize them by category in your pocket notebook.

5. Have you set a deadline? Make an appointment with yourself in your pocket calendar.

6. Have you allowed enough time to finish the job? Start at the finish line and walk backward.

7. Is your elephant a low-value task that you *have to* do? Identify a reward to spur you on, find a friend who will make you accountable, delegate the task, or let go of it.

8. Is it a high-value task that you *want to* do or *dream of* doing? Plan the reward that will follow its completion. Also consider doing it with a friend.

9. Have you scheduled your want-tos and dream-ofs in your prime time? If not, turn your day around as much as you can so your periods of high energy are devoted to high-value tasks.

10. If your elephant is a big, unpleasant job, like discarding the dead wood from your files, filing your tax return (or preparing the information for your accountant), or cleaning out the garage, have you agreed to do just a little each day over a longer time period? Decide ahead of time when you're going to stop, then ask a friend to make sure you do. Finally, enjoy a reward.

As I said in the Introduction, the extra inch, the difference between deciding to do something and doing it, is willpower. But what is willpower, and how do you get it?

I've heard it argued in human development seminars that a person must be *ready* to do something before he or she can do it. Well, that sounds like an oversimplified cliché, but as with most clichés, there's plenty of truth to it. If you have ever dieted and dieted and dieted, but finally lost weight and kept it off, you know that on the final try you were "ready." You may have thought about getting out of a horrible marriage for years, but you finally did so only when you were ready. And if you've ever left a bad job for a better one, you know that you moved to a greener pasture only once you felt ready to do so. So readiness is a factor, to be sure.

However, the testimony of hundreds who have taken my workshops has shown that willpower, or self-discipline, is fueled by the *successful completion of what you set out to do*. Recently a friend related this experience to me: "A few weeks ago, I got very depressed—my mountain of tasks seemed insurmountable. Then one night I said to myself, 'Okay, if nothing else, I promise to hang up my clothes every night for a week.' (I'd been so exhausted I'd just thrown things all over the place.) Well, that I could handle, and the funny thing was every night after I hung up my clothes, it was suddenly easy to do a little more—pay some bills, do some cleaning, etc. I'd only promised myself to do one simple task, but I was amazed how its accomplishment fueled my motivation to continue."

The more often you do a task that you have to do, want to do, or dream of doing, the easier it gets, especially with the added incentive of a planned reward. As I said in Day One, when you set a goal, perform one of the tasks, and reward yourself, you feel terrific, you boost your morale, and you feel ready to begin the next task. When you repeat this behavior pattern over time, self-discipline comes more easily to you and you have less trouble doing what you want to do. And self-discipline that comes more easily results in higher self-esteem for you!

Below you can follow three individuals as they learn the five-day method for getting organized and getting on with their lives. They are composites from my workshop participants, rather than real individuals, but their personal logjams, struggles, and successes are very real.

Gerry A.: Rebuilding a Social Life as a Widower

Gerry A., a 50-year-old real estate developer, lost his wife after her long struggle with cancer. They had no children. For more than a year Gerry has immersed himself in his work during the business day and has hidden inside his house after hours. Having had no interest in mixing with people, he has become a social recluse. But now, having passed through the worst of his grief, he feels ready to do something besides work. Gerry's "elephant" is to remake a social life for himself as a widower, that is, as a single man.

First Gerry thinks about rewards. He writes down the following:

Rewards

15 Minutes	*Two to Three Hours*	*Whole Day*
read	hike	golf
walk	read	
meditate		
swing a golf club		

Notice that Gerry has a hard time identifying rewards, especially for the larger blocks of time. Ever since his wife died, he's been a "couch potato" in front of his television. But his reward lists are a good start. More ideas will present themselves as he gets on with his life.

Gerry's brainstorm look like this:

Goal: Begin a Social Life

Go back to church

Give a party

Accept invitations to visit friends for the weekend

Read the daily paper for community events

Visit volunteer center re opportunities to do volunteer work

Call Jim re service clubs

Check out bridge lessons at the local Y

Tell Harry and Melissa I'll help with recycling program

Take partners and wives out to dinner

Call local hot line re support groups for widows and widowers

Tell Tom I'll be a tennis substitute

Some of the tasks on the list, like giving a party, are very frightening for Gerry. But thinking about that fear made him think about locating a support group, where he might be able to relate to others experiencing similar feelings. And Gerry remembers that in a brainstorm you write down everything you can think of. It's just a list. Nothing is carved in stone.

Next Gerry adds the tasks from his brainstorm to his pocket notebook. They break down like this:

Goal: Begin a Social Life

Calls

Jim re service clubs

Harry and Melissa re recycling

Hot line re support groups

Tom re tennis

Partners re dinner out

Make restaurant reservation

Newspaper for home delivery

Jeff and Nancy re weekend visit

Do

Plan a party

Read newspaper

Errands

Volunteer center

YMCA/YWCA re bridge

Church

Write

Gerry's tasks are all want-tos, (because his goal is a want-to) and as is often the case, no deadlines for them have been imposed by an outside source. It's up to Gerry to make his own deadlines so he can move forward and accomplish the goal of seeing old friends and making new ones.

Using his pocket calendar, Gerry finds some unscheduled time and makes appointments with himself to do a few of the tasks. He's understandably anxious about starting this new behavior, so the task he pulls from his notebook first is the call to the local hot line. He's not sure he'll join a support group, but he wants to know where and when it meets, just in case he gets "stuck."

Gerry's calendar for the next day looks like this:

Wednesday

8:00 A.M.	Breakfast meeting, Chamber of Commerce
9:30	On-site inspection of condominium project
11:00	Meeting with magazine ad rep
12:00 noon	Lunch with realtor re new land listings
1:30 P.M.	*Call hotline re support groups Walk around the block!
2:00	Review prospectus with marketing
3:00	Meet with architects
5:00	Go over materials with Carol for Planning & Zoning
7:30	Planning & Zoning meeting re Connors property

One could argue that Gerry's day is very lean on rewards, but it does show he's learning. Notice Gerry has made an appointment to call the hot line and followed it with a planned reward.

To complete the five-day method, Gerry makes his daily "to do" list for Wednesday first thing that morning. He starts with his calendar page and then adds tasks from his notebook. He also adds rewards.

Wednesday

8:00 A.M.	Breakfast meeting, Chamber of Commerce Go to newsstand for magazines Call courier service to pick up packages
9:30	On-site inspection of condominium project Coffee break!

11:00	Meeting with magazine ad rep
12:00 noon	Lunch with realtor re new land listings
1:30 P.M.	Call hot line re support groups
	Walk around the block!
2:00	Review prospectus with marketing
3:00	Meet with architects
	Call lawn care service, appliance repair
5:00	Go over materials with Carol for Planning & Zoning
	Read for pleasure!
	Stop at motor club office for new maps
7:30	Planning & Zoning meeting re Connors property

Most of Gerry's days are crowded with appointments and meetings, mostly have-tos, and stacked up, one after the other, they spell "burnout." However, Wednesday is markedly different from the rest. First, he completes a want-to task, which probably takes him no more than 10 minutes. Second, Gerry has added some rewards to his otherwise work-filled day. Most of the satisfaction he feels at the end of the day is the result of these two additions. Gerry is on his way.

Sarah J.: Getting Off the Merry-Go-Round

Sarah J., 28, is a marketing executive "on the way up" but totally out of control. Her creative ad copy has won her several awards, but she seldom meets a deadline on time, she's terrible about returning phone calls, and her office looks as if a tornado tore through it. Her colleagues have indulged her whirlwind work style, chalking it up to her absentminded-artist personality, but patience is wearing thin, as clients complaining about her delays are now going to the top. And Sarah too wants to get off the stressful merry-go-round she rides on constantly. She also wants to be successful in her career.

Sarah's goal, then, is to get control of her time, that is, to get organized. She begins by fantasizing about rewards. In reality, she never rewards herself, but being a creative type, she has no trouble inventing relaxing and diverting pastimes.

Rewards

15 Minutes	*Two to Three Hours*	*Whole Day*
relax in a hot tub	have a massage	go to a spa
read poetry	stare at the sea	explore a new place
have my palm read	climb trees	stay in bed and read
eat chocolate	float on a raft	visit with an old
ride a merry-go-round	build a snow fort	friend
	ride in a balloon	

Sarah's brainstorm looks like this:

Goal: Get Organized

Buy a pocket notebook

Buy a pocket calendar

Hire a professional organizer through the National Association of Professional Organizers

Get garbage bags for throwing away junk

Get file folders

Take everything off my desk—start from scratch!

Put everything I have to go through in one corner

Go through everything and enter tasks in pocket notebook—delegate everything I possibly can!—agree to do this two hours a day until it's done

Keep door to my office closed

Ask secretary to take phone messages and say I return calls after 3:00 P.M.

File only what I can't get from someone or somewhere else

Start a support group for people trying to get organized!

Leave work on time—ask Susan to come by and drag me away if necessary!

Enter all known deadlines in my calendar—"walk backward." If the deadline is unrealistic, extend it right away, not later

Brainstorm all my elephants

Label the tasks in my notebook as have-tos, want-tos, and dream-ofs

Ask John to make me accountable for daily rewards

Right now, "unplan" one weekend a month—cross it out on my calendar

Agree to be on time more often—when I am, have two rewards!

Go through my "in" box once a day with my secretary; delegate everything I can

Above is a brainstorm for getting organized at work, but unfortunately, Sarah didn't write it. I did. Sarah couldn't slow down long enough to list the bites to her elephant. She took my workshop and listed her wished-for rewards, but at first she chose *not* to use them to train herself to be organized.

Sarah continued accepting phone calls whenever they came in and routinely gave clients her home phone number, thereby extending her workday indefinitely. She also continued to schedule meetings back-to-back, not allowing enough preparation or travel time. Her office door still stood wide open at all times, inviting drop-in visitors to come in and chat. Suffice it to say she was not "ready" to get organized.

Two weeks later Sarah's boss gave her an ultimatum: get on top of her work and meet deadlines or find another job. Sarah was now forced to confront her lack of control and planning. Determined to succeed at getting organized she enlisted the help of her colleagues at work.

One friend helped her bite-size brainstorm all her elephants. Another helped her think of ways to cut down on interruptions. To make certain she planned and carried out rewards, again she asked her friends to help. She learned to leave the office for lunch and brief walks and to *plan* entertainment for several evenings each week. It took a crisis to motivate Sarah to change, but as a result, she's well on her way to getting, and staying, organized.

Elizabeth L.: Surviving the Stampede

Elizabeth L. is a young mother experiencing a stampede of elephants. She's 25 and the mother of two daughters, aged one and three. She completed two years of college before she left to marry and start her family. She has recently been divorced and Elizabeth has to find a job and child care in a hurry. She feels understandably overwhelmed.

Preoccupied by coping with her kids and making ends meet, Elizabeth insists she can't even fantasize about rewards. But because she has no choice except to get her act together and get going, she agrees to give the five-day method a try. She agrees to list how she would reward herself if she won the lottery.

Rewards

15 Minutes	*Two to Three Hours*	*Whole Day*
read	have my hair done	stay at the beach from sunup to sundown
take a nap	go shopping for evening clothes	
have my face made up	ride in a sailboat	have lunch and see live theater
be served high tea	go out to lunch	canoe down a gentle stream
take a walk	go to an art museum	
pick flowers		

Elizabeth has two distinct goals: to find a job and to find quality child care she can afford. She "eats" her elephants as follows:

Goal: Find a Job	**Goal: Find Child Care**
tell my friends I'm looking	tell my friends I'm looking
read the classifieds	read the classifieds
call employment agencies	call all town facilities listed in the yellow pages
check library resources for reentry programs for displaced homemakers that are free	call town department of social services re licensed home care
attend job fairs	call local sitter services
	call domestic and international au pair services
	place my own classified

Elizabeth quickly completes her brainstorming exercise but then realizes she also needs to write a résumé and buy some clothing suitable for work outside her home. She feels she's completely unskilled (what can she possibly write on her résumé?), she doesn't have any money for new clothes, and she wonders how she can conduct a job search while caring for two little girls. When her husband asked for a divorce, Elizabeth's already low self-esteem took another plunge, but she has to eat and pay the rent. She's determined to keep putting one foot in front of the other, taking one step at a time.

When Elizabeth organizes her tasks in her pocket notebook, the pages look like this:

Goals: Find a Job and Child Care

Calls	*Do*
Susan re job and child-care search	read classifieds every day
Martha "	
Jane "	
Helen "	
Barbara "	
employment agencies	
sitter services	
child-care centers	
department of social services	

Errands	*Write*
attend job fairs	résumé
check library	my own classified ad for child care
visit child-care centers	

When Elizabeth looks at the pages of her pocket calendar, they appear mostly blank, except for an occasional doctor appointment or family birthday to remember. Yet her days are long and full, spent in caring for her daughters. Just when she resolves to make internal appointments on her calendar, both daughters get sick. With a heavy heart and a dwindling bank account, Elizabeth resigns herself to a couple of write-off days.

When the kids are well, Elizabeth writes some tasks on her calendar. One day looks like this:

> *Thursday*
>
> draft résumé
>
> go to the library
>
> call Susan, Jane, and Helen

In between washing loads of laundry, preparing meals, entertaining her kids, and doing other housekeeping chores, Elizabeth feels the tasks above are reasonable goals for the day. She also notices something: getting organized and making plans feels good. She has more energy and actually looks forward to doing the tasks, which now seem so small compared to the larger elephants.

Elizabeth still has some juggling to do. She knows she can have real quiet time only when her kids are asleep, so she plans to draft her résumé while they nap in the afternoon. At the library she first indulges her daughters in the children's room, until they find some books that serve to amuse them while she does some research for herself. Afterward she rewards everyone for good behavior with an ice cream cone. Realizing how well the girls respond to the positive reinforcement, Elizabeth resolves to consider more seriously how she can give herself a planned reward after completing a task.

When someone asked Frank Gilbreth, the "efficiency expert" and beloved patriarch in *Cheaper by the Dozen*, what he wanted to save time *for*, he replied, "For work, if you love that best. For education, for beauty, for art, for pleasure. For mumblety-peg, if that's where your heart lies."

It's up to you. Do you want to climb out of your rut, to get out of first gear and do what you've always dreamed of doing? Or do you want to go along willy-nilly, as if you lived in that world of unlimited time, reacting to life rather than acting on it? If you want to get organized, *Five Days* shows you how to do so. Whether you stay organized and achieve your goals is up to you.

Notes

Notes

Notes